Wizoo Guide

Cubase Vst Plug-Ins

Ralf Kleinermanns

Cubase VST Plug-Ins

**The Best Software Effects
for VST Windows and Macintosh**

(:wizoo:)

Imprint

Publisher   Peter Gorges

Author   Ralf Kleinermanns

© Copyright 1999 by WIZOO midi, music & audio technology, Cologne, Germany
Printed in Belgium
ISBN 3-927954-33-0

Translation   Tom Green
Proofreading   Dave Bellingham
Layout and typesetting   Uwe Senkler, Hamburg
Cover design   design-box, Ravensburg
Printed by   Continental Printing/EGRA Grafik GmbH

Welcome ...

Not so long ago, the notion of a fully-fledged recording studio housed in a computer was, depending on your point of view, either a bold vision or a harebrained idea concocted by crackpots. Today, many musicians and producers would be lost without it.

Universally welcomed, this development was decisively influenced, if not—at a grass roots level—sparked, by Steinberg's ›Virtual Studio Technology.‹ Amazingly versatile, the impressive performance of Cubase Vst has to date won it well over 100,000 acolytes. It is now considered a standard.

A remarkable advantage of Vst is the option of expanding its on-board effects palette with plug-ins—add-on software, so to speak. The number of available effects is staggering, you are free to choose from countless alternatives for virtually every type of effect.

In this book, I have again done my best to avoid overkill on the techno-talk and keep the focus on our actual mission: making music and boning up on the tricks of the trade, and to this end, occasionally bend the blaze out of sounds. Plug-ins are just the tools to get the job done quickly, conveniently and in many cases intuitively, which is why they are among my favorite bits of virtual gear.

The facts and figures I'll share with you are of course good to know, but more than that, hopefully some of my enthusiasm for these boss gadgets will rub off on you.

Ralf Kleinermanns

Table of Contents

Table of Contents

Table of Contents

Wizoo Vst Guides Windows and Macintosh

First we'll talk about a different kind of plug, the obligatory gratuitous advertising type of plug: If you are a Vst newbie, be sure to check out the Wizoo Guides ›Vst Windows‹ or ›Vst Macintosh‹ for whatever system you happen to own.

Much of the basic Vst know-how that you'll need to make the most of plug-ins is treated in depth in these books. They will give you the bottom line on:

◆ the best computer and sound system hardware,

◆ determining and pushing the boundaries of performance limits,

◆ set up of busses and routing effects signals,

◆ pre- and post-fader modes,

◆ serial and parallel effects combinations,

◆ routing traps,

◆ internal Vst plug-ins,

◆ mixer automation,

◆ editing automation data,

◆ track bouncing,

◆ and whipping up special effects (e.g. gated/reverse reverb).

▶ For more info on the Wizoo Guides ›Cubase Vst Windows‹ and ›Cubase Vst Macintosh,‹ check out the catalog on Cd-Rom or at the Web site.

1 Basics

Without getting too philosophical, a bit of background info on the fundamental nature of plug-ins won't hurt. If you're losing sleep over unanswered questions such as, ›What exactly is a plug-in anyway?‹, ›Are all plug-ins created equal?‹, ›Where do all the little plug-ins come from?‹ and so forth, enlightenment is near.

What Is the Advantage of a Plug-in?

In contrast to regular software, which is inevitably equipped with too many or not enough features, the plug-in concept is a very user-friendly approach:

- ◆ The people who designed the software make up ground rules, so you don't have to deal with wildly divergent concepts.
- ◆ Expansions are pretty much limited to functions or features that every user expects something different from, so you can ›tailor‹ your plug-in arsenal to taste. And of course these little add-ons shouldn't further confuse an already complex program.

Hey, what do you know, the plug-in concept fits the bill…

What Is a Plug-in Anyway?

Although it doesn't take a degree in etymology to figure out, for the record, the term ›plug-in‹ was evidently inspired by the fact that this type of program is ›plugged in‹ to another. Thus a symbiosis of the ›parasitic‹—or rather, ›commensal‹

—plug-in software and the ›host‹ is created to upgrade the latter with additional features.

However, not everything that is touted as a ›modular expansion‹ can actually be called a plug-in. These little programs are distinguished by a few more attributes:

◆ A plug-in is a usually relatively small program module. For example, if you load a bunch of supplementary fonts to a word processing program, you wouldn't call this a ›plug-in‹ because a font set is really just a simple file.

◆ A plug-in manipulates functions or events through actual computation and expands the host program's range of functions. A simple printer driver or additional control fields for an operating system do not qualify as plug-ins.

◆ A plug-in does not run on its own. You can't start it separately, it needs the host program to ›survive.‹ You will always start a plug-in from the host program.

Once you understand what plug-ins are all about, it will make working with them so much easier. Although this probably sounds like something your fifth grade geometry teacher once harped on about, there are some facts you should be aware of:

Every active plug-in requires dedicated RAM and CPU performance. It has to run discreetly, but at the same time, communicate and be coordinated with other plug-ins. These are actually pretty demanding prerequisites—be sure to keep them in mind when you're working with plug-ins!

▶ Plug-ins are undercover operatives: Once installed, they look exactly like an inconspicuous but additional menu item. Don't be fooled, they're not! The remain independent ›program modules.‹ The only difference between a plug-in and a ›genuine program‹ is that the former is subordinate to the host program and cannot run on its own.

Many a VST newbie is taken aback when he or she discovers that fifteen plug-ins won't run simultaneously on an inherently slothful computer. They are unaccustomed to the fact that they can't call up the ›menu items‹ of a program at will and actually have to budget computing performance themselves.

It's in the nature of the beast that we tend to underestimate plug-ins, but this kind of misunderstanding is easily cleared up with a bit of fundamental knowledge.

Key Jargon

When you begin exploring the wild and wonderful world of plug-ins, you'll come across a number of terms which, in practice, are unfortunately not delineated all that clearly. To hold confusion to a manageable level, here's a quick rundown on the most important nomenclature:

Host

›Host‹ is the organism in which a parasite lives for nourishment or protection. Of course you could look at it more graciously and say the host software is a gregarious program such as Cubase Vst that welcomes other programs—such as Vst plug-ins that are unable to have a good time on their own—to the party. Only in the host's house can the plug-in do its song and dance.

Shell

›Shell‹ is of course a hard outer covering that a snail calls home, the armor of a turtle or the pesky stuff you have to crack before you can enjoy your pecans. In terms of software, a shell is the ›outer wrapping‹ for a plug-in.

The functionality of shells is, in essence, limited to enabling plug-ins to run. A real host such as Cubase Vst might be insulted if you called it a shell.

Platform

Originally the term referred to the different genera of computers such as the Apple Macintosh ›platform‹ as opposed to

The term ›shell‹ is used correctly by the plug-in maker Waves in conjunction with the Macintosh computer platform. Here the term describes an additional stage in the hierarchy, a level that does not actually have a true functionality but simply serves as a go-between for the Waves plug-ins and host software.

the Windows Pc ›platform.‹ Today the term is also used to distinguish operating systems and plug-in interfaces.

Like every other program, a plug-in is designed to run in just one computer world. Nevertheless, today the vast majority of plug-ins are available in Windows Pc as well as Macintosh versions. Often when you buy a program, you get both versions on a Cd-Rom—your computer automatically installs the appropriate version.

System Requirements

Here's another aspect that plug-ins share with ›normal‹ programs: It won't do to simply install a plug-in on any old computer with the appropriate operating system. Plug-ins, like full-blown programs, also have specific minimum performance specifications that a computer must measure up to— say something like ›166 MHz or higher Pentium.‹ They also require a relatively up-to-date operating system (e.g. Mac Os 7.6.1 or later, Windows 95/98). These specifications are called system requirements.

In a classic tail-wagging-the-dog scenario, the requirements for a plug-in can be substantially higher than those of the host software!

Interface

The plug-in must ›speak‹ a certain software language so that it can be integrated into the host software and exchange information with said host.

›Premiere‹ is a popular plug-in language for the Macintosh platform. If a plug-in ›speaks‹ this language, it is referred to as being in Premiere format. The host software is touted as featuring a Premiere interface. You'll find that your friendly sales rep or the box that the product comes in claims that both the plug-in and host software are ›compatible with Premiere‹ or ›support the Premiere platform.‹

Native

If the computations for a plug-in are executed exclusively by the computer's main processor (Cpu), it is called a ›native‹ plug-in, presumably because of this ›innate‹ ability.

There are however computer soundcards available featuring so-called ›Dsp capability.‹ A Dsp (**D**igital **S**ignal **P**rocessor) is a computer chip often used in specialized audio data computations. Some of the more popular systems featuring Dsp capabilities are DigiDesign ProTools, Lexicon Studio, Yamaha Dsp Factory and Creamware Pulsar and Scope.

Dsp systems do lighten the computer's load, but you should bear in mind that plug-ins have to be programmed specifically for this type of system. If you buy a native plug-in, you can't install just any Dsp soundcard and expect the card to execute the calculations for the plug-in.

A Dsp card can only generate on-board software effects or effects offered by third-party vendors.

Few plug-ins are offered by third-party vendors for Vst compatible Dsp systems, so we'll stick to discussing native plug-ins in this book. These are plug-ins that—if you own a relatively up-to-date Pc or Macintosh—you can run under Vst without requiring additional hardware.

Entities

In contrast to a hardware effects device, where unless daddy is a tycoon, you tend to run into physical limitations like ›I can only afford one,‹ you can actually clone a plug-in. For example, you can use a single plug in two Vst effects devices and have it—or more precisely it and it's twin—process different signals using different parameter settings. Those in the know say that several ›entities‹ of the plug-in are active.

Keep in mind that every active clone requires the full computing performance of the plug-in!

Realtime and Offline

Plug-ins can run in two different modes, realtime and offline. Knowing the difference between these is essential when you're using plug-ins to whip audio tracks into shape:

Realtime

This is the most common option for running plug-ins in VST. If you play back an audio track and use an audio plug-in to compute a reverb effect ›online,‹ then this plug-in is running in realtime.

In this mode, the plug-in computes all audio data ultra-quickly (more or less) and is able to generate and output the effects signal (very nearly) simultaneously. It doesn't have to store effects data first and ›forget‹ what it was that it just computed. In other words, you can hear the effect as soon as the plug-in has calculated without having to save this data and listen to it later.

Offline

In a sample editing application, on the other hand, you'll generally you select an audio waveform, start the plug-in to calculate the effect and then wait for a spell while it figures out what you were up to. Only when it has finished can you hear the effect. It may not be earth-shattering news to you, but this process is executed in anything but realtime. This ›buy-now-fly-later‹ type of operation is executed ›offline.‹

Here the plug-in is unable to get the job done ›online:‹ First it loads a tidbit of audio from the hard disk to the RAM of the computer. It computes the effect and writes the results back to hard disk. Then once the RAM is vacated, it can load the next audio morsel and so forth.

In offline mode, the plug-in has to write data that it computes to disk, which is why it as often called a ›disk,‹ ›file-based‹ or even a ›destructive‹ process.

Why ›destructive,‹ because you'll work yourself into a petulant frenzy and break stuff when all this piecemeal processing takes too long? No, actually because in the dark days of digital audio the original file was usually overwritten by the generated effects file. Today however, all reasonably up-to-date programs offer the option of generating a new effects audio file so that the original file remains intact.

Before you enter the final command for an offline plug-in to compute the effects files, you can usually listen to the aural product of the current parameter settings in isolation. This option is often accurately called a ›preview‹ by the masterminds who designed the plug-ins. You can only preview a brief segment of the audio file—to be precise, exactly the amount of data that the RAM assigned to the plug-in can hold.

As a rule, all VST compatible plug-ins can operate in realtime in VST, provided of course your computer can deliver the performance required to execute the calculations.

Whether or not a plug-in can operate in realtime depends primarily on the plug-in format, although sometimes the type of host program is a factor.

A Brief Look Back

If we indulge in a quick retrospective of the early development of the first audio plug-ins, we'll come across a couple of ›familiar faces,‹ which will give us some insight into the origins and brains trust of a software house or two.

The notion caught on in the late 80s, possibly being the coolest thing that this taste-challenged decade produced. Back then, two totally distinct avenues of approach were pursued by different companies:

◆ In Tennessee, a company called Audio Animation developed a product, the unpretentiously-named Paragon. This was the first user-programmable DSP box. The system featured 64 signal busses with all the key processing tools (e.g. EQ, compressor, limiter, stereo imager, reverb).

21

▶ Audio Animation had to close shop in 1991. However, many of the people who contributed to the development of Paragon are today in the employ of the market leader among plug-in makers, the Israeli company Waves.

◆ In the vapor trail of a research project, the Us communications giant Bell Labs developed a technology that they called ›Time Division Multiplexing,‹ TDM if you're in a hurry. The company Spectral Synthesis used it to come up with a marketable product called Audioscape, a Pc-based system with 256 audio busses. Here too, users and third-party vendors had a special software available that enabled them to access the DSP of the system in realtime and thus program their own effects.

▶ Spectral met a considerably less cruel fate than their competitor Audio Animation—today the company is a division of Euphonix, a successful manufacturer of digital mixing consoles.

Paradoxically, these plug-in pioneers have been relegated to near obscurity, primarily because another company, Digidesign, managed to turn this great idea into coinage.

In 1989, its stereo HD recording system Sound Tools for Macintosh debuted. Digidesign—in collaboration with Apple—borrowed heavily from the two concepts discussed earlier and developed the first commercially successful audio plug-in interface for the Sound Tools editor software, Sound Designer II.

On a roll, Digidesign went ahead and released the first plug-in for Sound Designer II. The denoiser plug DINR (›**DI**gital **N**oise and Hum **R**eduction‹) immediately had the industry abuzz. Although priced around $ 1,000, it put a substantial dent in the average allowance, the plug was nevertheless a bargain. Systems that were able deliver a comparable level of quality while purging noise and hum from audio tracks cost at least ten times this amount.

Next the original version of an equalizer plug-in, the successor of which is still available today, the Q10, was released.

It was the first Sound Designer II plug-in available from a third-party vendor, coincidentally none other than Waves.

In 1994, the evolution of plug-ins made a giant stride forward when Digidesign introduced a hard- and software expansion for their high-end HD recording system ProTools. It was based on the technology developed by Bell Labs mentioned on earlier. Cunningly, Digidesign came up with the rather brazen name ›Trans-System **D**igital **M**atrix‹ for their version, which, remarkably(!), is also abbreviated to TDM.

In any rate, ProTools TDM was the first multitrack music production system with a virtual mixer, flexible signal routing and plug-in interfaces. It also required relatively expensive DSP hardware cards to work all of this magic, a situation which hasn't changed an iota since.

In 1995, with the release of the ›Virtual Fx Rack Vol. 1‹ software package, Steinberg was one of the first companies to offer TDM plug-ins.

You know the rest: In 1996, Steinberg's Cubase VST premiered for the Macintosh. It was, in principle, comparable to TDM systems, with one huge difference—you didn't have to shell out mega-bucks for additional DSP hardware. Thus began the native plug-ins' campaign of world domination, and in terms of numbers and selection, this breed of plug-in remains the market leader.

2 VST: A Hands-on Primer

Now that we've explored the origins of plug-ins, we'll take a closer look at their ramifications for Cubase VST. Our primary concern is, of course, which plug-in formats are compatible with VST and what should you be aware of when you're looking at a given format.

Mac Format: VST Macintosh

Let's begin with the Macintosh, because here the situation couldn't be clearer. Unsurprisingly, VST Macintosh supports solely the inhouse plug-in format ›VST Macintosh.‹

This doesn't mean that you are dealing with what Joe Computer would call an island solution. Hugely popular, the widespread appeal of VST Macintosh is making this plug-in format a standard. Today many VST Macintosh-compatible plug-ins run in the current versions of other host programs, for instance:

- Emagic ›Logic Audio‹
- Opcode ›Vision DSP‹
- Prosoniq ›SonicWORX Studio‹
- Cakewalk ›Metro‹

Cubase VST, however, has what we'll call the ›home team‹ advantage simply because the program was fine-tuned to interact with a plug-in interface designed specifically for it. Currently, VST Macintosh plug-ins are substantially more stable in CubaseVST and require less computing power than in other applications.

You can bet that the programmers of these other manufacturers are hard at work trying to rectify this situation, but wether or not the ›foreign‹ software will ever be able to match the performance of Cubase VST is, for now, debatable. If you are planning on buying the plug-in of your dreams first and *then* the host software as an afterthought, be sure to keep this in mind.

Macintosh VST plug-ins are often easily identifed by a red icon resembling a 1/4" jack (see the illustration at the top), but there are exceptions (see the illustration at the bottom). If you select this type of file and then press ⌘ⅰ on the computer keyboard, the info box under KIND will generally display a comment such as ›Cubase VST document.‹

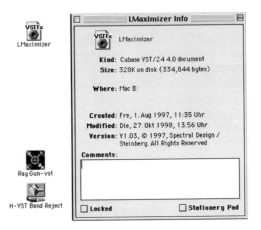

Windows Format 1: VST PC

The inhouse plug-in format for VST Windows is predictably called ›VST PC.‹ In principal, the same observations made on the VST Macintosh format hold true for VST PC. This is the best plug-in interface for Cubase VST Windows simply because it doesn't get more ›native‹ than this—the same company that made the host program designed the interface. Here you don't have to worry about any contingencies whatsoever, the program runs just fine and the load on the computer is as light as the programmers—who have in-depth insight into every detail of the host program—can possibly make it.

Apart from Cubase VST, there is currently just one Windows-based host application that supports this format, Steinberg's WaveLab (Version 2.0 and later). However, Steinberg recently granted licenses for its plug-in interfaces as well as Asio technology to third-party vendors, so you can be sure that other host programs will soon follow.

▶ A Vst Pc plug-in is always a file with the extension ›.dll‹ (Dll = **D**y-namic **L**ink **L**ibrary) following the file name. In the standard setup, Windows displays a page with two gear icons as a symbol for this type of ›program library.‹

DPole.dll

Windows Format 2: DirectX

In addition to the in-house Vst Pc format, Cubase Vst Windows supports another plug-in interface which today is generally called ›DirectX.‹

Not merely an audio plug-in format, Microsoft DirectX is actually a package of software interfaces. Primarily designed for programming games, it enables programmers direct, and thus very fast, access to computer hardware such as 3-D graphics cards, joysticks and soundcards.

If you want to use audio plug-ins in DirectX format, the Microsoft DirectX package has to be installed on your computer. This is something akin to an operating system expansion without which you cannot deploy DirectX-compatible soft- and hardware.

If you're the proud owner of Windows 98, you won't have to worry about installing DirectX, Mr. Gates and his minions kindly integrated DirectX into the operating system.

If you own a Windows 95 system, you'll have to install DirectX yourself. If you're interested, you can find the software on

This format is the source of much confusion, a situation which Microsoft helped bring about. Today it is usually referred to as ›DirectX,‹ but its former official designations ›Active-Movie‹ and ›Direct-Show‹ tend to crop up every now and then.
Don't let the name game bother you, in terms of audio plug-ins, they all refer to the same format.

- ◆ your Windows Cd—provided it is the Win 95B version,
- ◆ Microsoft's Internet server at
  http://www.microsoft.com/
- ◆ the Cubase Vst Cds or
- ◆ the Cd-Rom included with this book in the folder Helpers.

Steinberg recommends DirectX Version 5.1 and later.

▶ Caution: Before you install DirectX, make absolutely certain that your sound- and graphics card(s) are ›DirectX-compatible.‹ This is standard today, but experience has proven that some older computer components are incompatible with DirectX. In these cases, installing DirectX may cause your computer system to crash more often, or—in worst-case scenarios—not boot at all!

In this book, the terms ›VST PC plug-in‹ always refer to the in-house VST PC format, never DirectX. When you're shopping for plug-ins, you may find that a DirectX plug-in—because it is compatible with VST Windows—is labelled a ›VST‹ or ›VST Windows plug-in.‹ Keep in mind that these are apples and oranges. If you're unsure which format the plug-in is actually in, don't hesitate to ask. Read on and you'll find that there are some very significant differences between the two.

DirectX is a widely accepted plug-in format for Windows PCs, so the selection is huge. Aside from VST Windows, it is supported by the following host software, among others:

◆ Steinberg ›WaveLab‹

◆ Sonic Foundry ›Sound Forge‹

◆ Sonic Foundry ›Acid‹

◆ Syntrillium ›Cool Edit Pro‹

◆ CakeWalk ›Pro Audio‹

◆ Emagic ›Logic Audio Windows‹

◆ SEKD ›Samplitude 2498‹

◆ Waves ›WaveConvert Pro‹

VST PC Vs. DirectX

Reasonably, for VST Windows, the DirectX plug-in interface is more or less an ›alien body,‹ at least in comparison to the more familiar inhouse VST PC interface. When you pit the two formats against each other in a head-to-head shootout, you'll find that DirectX plug-ins under VST Windows have two tremendous disadvantages:

◆ PERFORMANCE: When a software maker programs DirectX as well as VST PC versions of a plug-in and does an excellent job of both, according to Steinberg, the performance of the VST PC plug-in under VST Windows is some 10 % better than that of the DirectX plug-in. While executing identical operations, the VST PC version would thus place 10 % less load of the processing power required by the plug-in on the computer's CPU.

◆ PARAMETER AUTOMATION: You can automate parameters in VST when you're using plug-ins in the inhouse VST PC and VST Macintosh formats (see page 39). With DirectX plug-ins under Cubase VST Windows, you'll have to pass on this extremely practical and hugely fun option.

This doesn't mean that DirectX plug-ins are taboo for use in Cubase VST Windows: This interface is extremely dependable and gives good performance, so other than these two exceptions, you can use it without reservation.

Nevertheless, if you're a Windows user and are forced to choose between two comparable plug-ins—only one of which is available in a VST PC version, my advice is to choose it over the DirectX version.

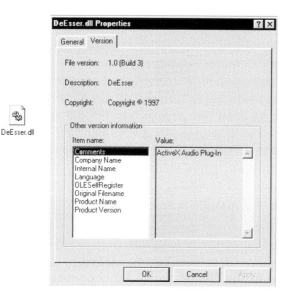

Usually, a DirectX plug-in is also actually a DLL file. If you're unsure of what you're dealing with—the DirectX or VST PC format—you can often find out under PROPERTIES in the FILE menu (click on the file via the right mouse button ⇨ PROPERTIES ⇨ VERSION).

Installation Tips

If you want to expand your VST system with a new plug-in, installation is usually executed automatically via aptly-named ›installer software.‹ All you need to do is indicate the location of the VST program folder on the hard disk—the rest of the procedure is knocked out automatically.

▶ Say you've downloaded a plug-in from the Internet and it doesn't look anything like the description in the previous section, you're probably looking at a ›compressed file format.‹ A sure sign of a compressed file is a file name with the extension zip, sit or hqx. In this case, you first have to ›unpack‹ the plug-in via some type of decompression software. Nico Mak ›Winzip‹ for Windows PCs and Aladdin ›StuffIt Expander‹ for Macintosh are standard programs used for this purpose. You'll find these utilities in the Helpers folder on the included CD-ROM.

Consider manual installation a last resort. If a plug-in features installation software, definitely use it, particularly when you're dealing with DirectX plug-ins!

On the other hand, if you're dealing with freeware or demo plug-ins from the Internet or off a CD-ROM that do not come complete with installation software, the process is not nearly as convenient and simple. Depending on the plug-in format, proceed as follows:

◆ VST PC/Macintosh: The procedure is simple enough for the inhouse VST plug-in formats. All you have to do is copy or drag and drop the plug-in into the folder VSTPlugIns (Macintosh) or VSTplugins (Windows PC). This folder is always located in the Cubase-VST program folder.

▶ All plug-ins must be archived in this Macintosh or Windows folder. Even when you load a bundle featuring a bunch of individual plug-ins (e.g. Hyperprism VST), you may not group these in subordinate folders—if you do, VST will not be able to locate the plug-ins.

Heads up, Macintosh users: There are two different WaveShells, one for VST Macintosh versions to 3.52, the other for VST 4.0 and higher.

If you're dealing with VST Macintosh plug-ins by Waves, disregard the above: Here only the ›WaveShell-VST‹ plug-in has to be located in the central folder. It automatically accesses the individual Waves plug-ins which may reside in any shared folder on the hard disk.

♦ DIRECTX: In contrast to the other formats, DirectX plug-ins do not have to be collated centrally in a VST subfolder. Generally for this breed of plug-ins, a separate folder for each plug-in vendor is generated on the hard disk; the maker's DirectX plug-ins are loaded to the appropriate folder. Where you file a DirectX plug-in is entirely up to you.

▶ A DirectX plug-in must be ›registered‹ separately for each host program. Normally the installer software will take care of this automatically. If you have copied a ›naked‹ DirectX plug-in without installer software to your hard disk, you have to register it manually for VST. Simply drag the plug-in DLL file to the VST program icon or an appropriate link to start VST.

You only have to do this once for each DirectX plug-in. However, afterwards you may not move the plug-in to another location on the hard disk.

As usual, not all installation procedures are created equal—you will find the odd exotic application that demands a different song and dance. For example, VST Macintosh plug-ins by Spectral Designs require an additional ›Engine‹ file that must be located in a subfolder titled Spectral Designs Plugs.eff in the VSTPlugIns folder. Other exceptions include Opcode and Arboretum products. Fortunately, here an installer loads the programs to hard disk for you, so generally you won't have to worry about the installation details.

Editing Parameters via a Computer Keyboard

Most commercial plug-ins work with a dedicated, relatively comfortable graphical user interface. Rather than the ALPHA DIAL, the VST effects devices display an EDIT button that lets you call up a dialog box.

The faders and knobs that grace these interfaces generally look great, but you'll find that it's much easier and faster, not to mention more precise, to enter values via your computer keyboard. How you go about entering parameter values in this manner—and if it is possible at all—depends on the plug-in, VST version, presets, as well as the area of the computer keyboard that you're able to work with.

In my experience, the following standard method seems to work best:

Some plug-ins (e.g. Waves) seem slightly allergic to values entered via computer keyboard. Occasionally, you won't be able to exit the parameter box via the ⏎, *tab* or mouse button. In these cases, *esc* usually does the trick.

◆ In VST (Windows only), deactivate the menu item PLUGINS RECEIVE KEY COMMANDS under FILE ⇨ PREFERENCES. This command influences the behavior of the numeric keypad on the computer keyboard, which in VST isn't particularly well-suited for controlling plug-ins because several keys are almost always reserved for VST tape transport functions.

◆ Attempt to activate numeric parameters for your plug-ins via a double-click and type in parameters using the numeric keys on the typewriter keyboard. If you get lucky this will work, most of the time it won't.

This aspect of plug-in handling in VST is currently too inconsistent to even come close to being satisfactory. In most cases, you'll have to settle for entering parameters via the available graphical control features.

Small is beautiful: Only when a VST effects device resembles the device at the right is it home to a plug-in with its own graphical user interface.

Editing Parameters via the Mouse

In many of the plug-ins that ship with VST—and most of the freeware plug-ins—you'll search in vain for the magic EDIT button. These plug-ins rely on the less than convenient standard control features of the ›virtual effects devices.‹

To modify these plug-ins' parameters in small increments, you have but one option:

1   Position the effects device that you want to edit at the center of your screen.

2   Use the mouse to select the parameter that you want to change.

3   Move the cursor to the ALPHA DIAL located to the right of the display. Do not however place the cursor directly over it, instead press and hold the mouse button to drag it to the far edge of the screen.

4   Now drag the cursor down the edge of the screen. This method lets you access every increment of a parameter very easily.

Better House-keeping: Archiving Plug-ins

If you are the hunter-and-gatherer type, or worse, a notorious pack rat, you will find yourself installing plug-ins that you use about as often as Halley's Comet comes around. These ›sleepers‹ tend to clutter your VST effects selection menus. What's more, if the plug-in is the product of what we'll leniently call ›dodgy‹ programming, it may destabilize your VST system.

I recommend that you install only those plug-ins that you really need ›properly‹ and ›park‹ the rest somewhere handy where you can retrieve them if need be. It only takes a minute and leaves your menus looking tidy enough to make Mom proud:

◆   VST Macintosh/PC: Go to the VST program folder and in addition to the ›official‹ plug-in folder, generate another folder. Call it ›VST Plugs Depot,‹ ›Plug Purgatory‹ or something similar and drag and drop all of the plugs gathering virtual dust to this repository.

▶   Be sure to keep the exceptions discussed in the previous section in mind when you're playing musical plug-ins, especially if you're a Macintosh user. If a plug-in features a Help file and you want to hang onto it just in case, you should move it along with the file it belongs to.

◆ DIRECTX: Rejoice because here it's even easier to rid your menus of pesky loiterers. VST Windows features a menu item that lets you hide DirectX plug-ins:

1   Go to the AUDIO menu and select the item DIRECTX PLUGINS.

2   A box opens that displays all DirectX plug-ins installed on your computer. If you want to temporarily deactivate certain plug-ins, click on the little box at the left of the line listing the name of a plug so that the check mark in it disappears.

3   VST will kindly leave these settings as they are until you decide to change them.

The DirectX plug-in box in VST Windows: In the first column, you can deactivate individual plugs for VST; the second column indicates how often a plug-in is activated in the current song.

In the effects selection menu of VST Windows, you can view the different formats of the installed plug-ins. The top section of the pop-up menu under NO EFFECT lists the VST PC plug-ins, the bottom block the DirectX plug-ins.

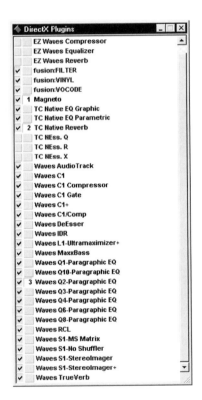

Inexplicably, with some Internet browsers, you may find that their expansions end up as DirectX plug-ins in your VST system, where of course they don't belong. If your VST computer also has Internet access software installed to it, be sure to check this box in VST Windows every now and then to purge these ›trespassers.‹

Saving and Loading Plug-in Settings

VST automatically stores the parameter settings of all plug-ins used in a song along with the song file. This also holds true for the settings of plugs in a deactivated VST effects device. In other words, you don't have to worry about saving specific plug-in settings.

If you want to dial in the settings of a plug-in separately and later load these to a song, however, you will have to save them manually. For simple plug-ins such as WunderVerb 3, you probably won't need this option. For more complex plugs featuring loads of parameters, I recommend that you compile a library of your own effect programs over time. This is how you go about archiving effects settings:

1   Set all parameters of the plug-in as desired.

2   Click on the top line of the display for the VST effects device; its default should read INIT. Now you can enter any term that you care to—the effects program will henceforth be indicated by this name.

3   Click on the entry FILE at the right and select SAVE EFFECT. Now you can save the effects program as a separate file anywhere on the hard disk.

▶   Note: The name that appears in the display of the effects devices is not automatically identical to the name of the file. It you want the two to be the same, you have to type the name in again when you save the file, which is probably a good idea to avoid turning your library into an administrative nightmare!

4   Once an effects program has been saved in this manner, you can load it back to the plug-in at any time. Simply select FILE ⇨ LOAD EFFECT. The previously selected PROGRAM is overwritten.

Obviously, a plug-in can only load its own effects programs. For instance, you can't load an effects program to ›GrooveDelay Xт‹ that you saved in ›GrooveDelay.‹ Ergo, if a plug-in fails to respond when you try to load an effects program that you saved previously, the most likely explanation is that you saved the program in another plug-in.

To avoid these kinds of glitches, I suggest you establish some type of filing system for your effects programs. The following works well enough for me:

♦ In the ›VsтPlugIns‹ folder, generate a folder for every installed plug-in. In future, file all of the plug-in's effects programs in it—but not however the actual plug-in!

Some plug-ins automatically generate this type of folder during installation. In Vsт Windows for example, a folder called Espacialfx is generated, in Vsт Macintosh it is named ESpacial.eff. Some plug-ins automatically add Presets to the folder name.

How you go about administering your effects programs is entirely up to you, but I do recommend that you use a uniform system that makes it easy to find what you're looking for.

♦ It is a good idea to precede every file name of an effects program with initials or an abbreviation indicating which plug-in was used to create the program, for instance for GrooveDelay, ›Gд 1/8 Feedback,‹ for GrooveDelay Xт, ›Gд_xт 1/8 Feedback.‹ This avoids the kind of tearing-your-hair-out-at-the-roots frustration that comes with looking for something that you just can't find.

▶ For quick access to the ›VsтPlugIns‹ folder and the plugs and effects settings contained therein, I recommend that you place an icon linked to this folder directly on the desktop:
Windows-Pc: Drag the folder to the desktop via the right mouse button and select CREATE SHORTCUT.
Macintosh: Select the folder and using ⌘Ⓜ, generate an alias. Drag it to the desktop.

In Vsт Windows Version 3.6 and higher, a bar that provides direct access to an On/Off button, PROGRAM selector and display as well as the FILE commands is located at the top of each plug-in parameter box.

In Vsт Macintosh 4.0, you still have to use the control features of the effects rack.

Managing Effects Banks

Like most hardware effects processors, Vsт effects devices can also administer several effects programs in groups. Here you have to distinguish between two types of data:

◆ PROGRAM (or EFFECT) refers to an individual effects preset described in the section above.

◆ BANK refers to a groups of these PROGRAMS or presets.

▶ A Vsт effects device can administer a maximum of sixteen PROGRAMS in a BANK. If you are able to actually load this number of PROGRAMS to a BANK depends on the type of plug-in that they were created in. Some plug-ins can only handle BANKS with up to eight PROGRAMS. In other plug-ins (e.g. Waves Macintosh) a BANK can only contain a single PROGRAM.

On the Vst effects device, you can navigate among the different PROGRAMS of the currently selected bank via the PROGRAM UP/DOWN keys. The display always indicates the current PROGRAM number in the second line (PROG 1 to PROG 16). You have two practical options for loading data to a BANK:

◆ Select PROGRAM 1 and edit it, go to PROGRAM 2 and edit it and so forth.

A BANK is particularly handy when you want a plug-in's settings to change automatically during the course of a song (see page 39).

◆ Select PROGRAM 1, load an individual program that you saved previously to this slot (LOAD EFFECT), go to PROGRAM 2, load another individual program etc.

You can freely combine these two methods and load programs in any sequence that you desire. In other words, you can go to any PROGRAM number within the BANK at random.

All changes that you make to the diverse PROGRAMS of a BANK remain intact until you change the plug in this effects device or deactivate it via No EFFECT. Switching the effects devices off via the POWER button does not delete the changes that you made.

When you save a PROGRAM, Vst Windows automatically adds the extension ›.fxp‹ (**Fx P**ROGRAM) to the file name and ›.fxb‹ (**Fx B**ANK) to a BANK. If you so desire, you can go to the Windows system settings and assign different symbols to the two file types (VIEW ⇨ OPTIONS ⇨ FILE TYPES ⇨ NEW TYPE).

When you save a song, you are not only saving the current PROGRAM of each active plug-in, but also the contents of the entire BANK. Bear in mind that if you've edited several programs within a BANK before saving a song, all PROGRAMS will retain the status that they had when you last saved them, when the song is next loaded.

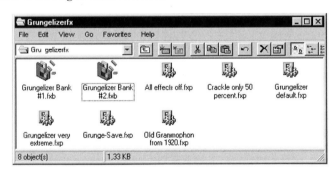

Saving a BANK as a separate file is thus only a feasible when you want to archive it for later use in a song or expand it bit by bit.

The process is the same as with the PROGRAMS, except that the FILE commands are SAVE BANK and LOAD BANK.

By the way, you can save BANK files along with the PROGRAM files in a specific plug-in effects folder. Even if the folder contains two disparate file types, the program will display PROGRAM files only in response to a LOAD EFFECT command and BANK files only after LOAD BANK.

In VST Macintosh, you can easily distinguish between PROGRAM and BANK files by simply looking at the icons—›FxPrg‹ always indicates a PROGRAM and ›FxBnk‹ a BANK.

▶ In addition to the standard VST methods of administering plug-in PROGRAMS and BANKS that we just had a look at, some plugs-ins (e.g. Waves) feature file management utilities. You can choose which option you prefer.

However, keep in mind that the file formats of the standard VST file management and the plug-in's internal file utility are not interchangeable.

Dynamic Parameter Automation

Most VST users exploit the VST mixer automation feature for volume level and panorama control only. Fair enough, but you can also use it to automate plug-in-parameters in VST PC or VST Macintosh.

In contrast to VST PC and VST Macintosh plug-ins, DirectX plug-in cannot be automated in VST!

Here's how it goes:

1 Even if you are planning to use the effect later on in the song, be sure to activate the effects device before you record an automation sequence, otherwise VST will not register its presets.

2 Set the plug-in-parameters to the values that you want it to have when the song starts.

3 Set VST to the start of the song and activate WRITE located at the top left of the AUDIO MIXER.

4 Play the song (PLAY mode) and change the plug-in-parameters as you see fit.

5 After you're finished, stop the virtual tape transport, deactivate the WRITE button, and activate the READ button.

6 Now VST should automatically execute the parameter changes that you made on the plug-in. If you're dissatisfied with the results, you can activate the WRITE along with the READ button and overwrite your automation data by repeating Steps 4 and 5.

The number of parameters that you can automate is limited internally by VST to sixteen per plug-in. Most plug-in makers exploit this option's full potential, but it won't suffice to automate all parameters of a truly complex plug-in such as an EQ with loads of bands.

Switching Effects Automatically

You feel that automating plug-in parameters is a bit over-the-top? Expanding reverb rooms, delay modulations and similar trickery is not your cup of tea?

Fair enough, but consider that no matter how down-to-earth you like your mixdown to be, there is one plug-in parameter that can do with a pinch of automation in even the most conservative mix—that's right, the PROGRAM number. You can thus switch the settings of an entire plug-in automatically. Here the static method of defining an automation setup is usually best:

1 Activate the plug-in and set up a BANK with all of the individual PRO-GRAMS that you need for a song (see page 35).

2 Select the desired PROGRAM for the start of the SONG.

3 Set the Play cursor to the start of the song, but leave the program in STOP mode.

4 Click on the WRITE button in the VST Audio Mixer once and switch the WRITE function right back off again.

5 Set the Play cursor to a position just prior to the song position at which you want to change the PROGRAM number.

6 Select the new PROGRAM number on the plug-in. Switch the WRITE function on and right back off again.

7 Repeat Steps 5 and 6 for all desired PROGRAM changes.

8 When you're finished, switch the WRITE function off and the READ function on. Now activate PLAY and review your work—are all of the PROGRAM changes executed at the right positions?

The unusual thing about this technique is that VST remains in STOP mode for the duration of the automation programming procedure. Every time you switch the WRITE function on and back off again, VST ›photographs‹ the automation setting and saves this snap-shot at the current song position.

There are two more considerations you should keep in mind when you're working this way:

◆ Only switch PROGRAMS at positions where the plug-in is not receiving an input signal. Otherwise, most plug-ins tend to respond with an audible switching noise or similarly undesirable sonic side effect.

◆ It takes a certain amount of time for the plug-in to resume normal noise-free operations after it has received a program change command. Unfortunately, you'll have to find out for yourself how long this brief interval is because it depends on the computer, soundcard, driver interface, latency, plug-in and for all I know, the relative humidity.

◆ Once you become more experienced with your system, be sure to keep this factor in mind when you're positioning PROGRAM changes.

Idle Effects—The Performance Parasites

If you're running Cubase Vst on a computer that just barely meets the minimum system requirements, you don't have any performance ›headroom.‹

In this case you many find that the appetite of Cpu-hungry plug-ins is greater than the calories that your system can provide—it will give you serious realtime grief. You'll know what the deal is when it does the breakfast cereal thing—snap, crackle and pop—stalls, or crashes altogether when attempting to compute an effect.

The bad news is that it's impossible to say exactly where the threshold at which your box will start acting up lies, the good news is that this type of problem can easily be avoided if you know how:

▶ Once you select a plug in a Vst effects rack, it is ›initialized‹ even if the effects device to which it is loaded is switched off. Like a hardware device on standby requires some power, active effects in inactive effects devices always require some Ram and Cpu resources!

▶ This ›idle load‹ is identical for all plug-ins, which means that the—in terms of performance requirements—extremely miserly WunderVerb 3 consumes up as much computing power as the wastrel Waves True-Verb.

To be honest, the additional load on the computer through initialized plug-ins is relatively insignificant. Be aware though that Vst's internal Cpu Performance meter does not indicate the increased load, it is tangible. If you ›idle‹ many effects devices at once, these add up and your computer will ›feel‹ the crunch. Especially when you're already pushing the performance limits of your box, these sleepers may make the difference between a plug-in that runs cleanly and one that sounds as if it about to self-destruct. Nip the problem at the bud and try to make a habit of setting all inactive effects devices to No Effect!

Transcending Performance Limits

Note: An inactive effects device with a selected effect (at the top) nibbles at your computer's CPU and RAM-resources, while the setting NO EFFECT (bottom) leaves well enough alone.

It your computer's CPU performance is too low to ensure flawless realtime operation of a plug-in, you can always have the computer calculate the effect offline. In this mode, VST scoffs at the performance specifications of your sloth-slow box and computes sophisticated effects in impeccable quality despite the computer's sluggishness:

1 First, mute all tracks except for the one you want to work with. Deactivate all plug-ins other than the one that deliver the effect that you want.

2 Set the effects parameters as desired.

3 In ARRANGE, set the left locator to precisely the position where the first SEGMENT of the audio track that you want to edit begins. Set the right locator slightly after the end of the last SEGMENT of this track.

4 Click on the EXPORT AUDIO button in the MASTER B strip. When the corresponding box opens, check if the option EFFECTS/MASTER EFFECTS is active. If not, click on it to make sure that the plug-in actually influences the signal.

5 Click on SAVE. This generates a new audio file containing the original signal of the ›open‹ audio track including the effect. This is how a digital recording of the VST Master output signal would sound if your computer had enough horsepower to compute the plug in realtime.

6 You can import this file to VST and use it along with or instead of the original file in the ARRANGEMENT.

The entire process is rather cumbersome; so consider it a last resort resolution. However, if you're dead-set on using a special combination of plug-ins that your computer can't handle in realtime, it will get the job done.

Using Foreign Plug-ins in VST

Say that you've been messing around with plug-ins for a while and find them nifty enough. You discover a new plug: affordable, killer sound, hip interface, unique effects—in short, a dream come true!

Uncontrollable gear-lust drives you to whip out your wallet or rip open your purse, but before you hand over the greenbacks, you take a gander at the compatibility list: no VST Macintosh, no VST PC, no DirectX format—your dream just turned into an nightmare!

Breathe deep and stay cool: This scenario is relatively unlikely—Cubase VST is a very popular host application and few plug-in vendors can afford to ignore it.

This is particularly relevant if you run the program on Windows, where you'll be on the safe side with the VST PC and DirectX formats. For this reason,Cubase VST Windows users can skip the remainder of this section.

On the Macintosh platform, there are two other popular ›native‹ plug-in formats alongside the VST Macintosh plug-in interface:

AudioSuite

This is a native plug-in format that was developed by Digidesign. Currently it works offline only, but it does have an unusual feature: you can select several files and process them simultaneously.

▶ For example, the AudioSuite LoFi by Digidesign is a hip plug-in package that is currently unavailable in VST Macintosh format. It consists of four separate plugs that let you come up all kinds of wild effects from retro and sci-fi sounds to tape-stop effects at a level of quality worth drooling over.

Premiere

This native plug-in format was developed by Adobe. Premiere is also designed for offline operation, but this standard is more open so that some host programs are able to expand the program's options.

► A totally unique plug-in—currently only available as a Premiere version—is the Bias Sfx Machine. This is a modular effects kit that lets you construct your own effects processors based on its diverse modules. For the creative Diy sound alchemist, this is one of the hippest plug-ins available!

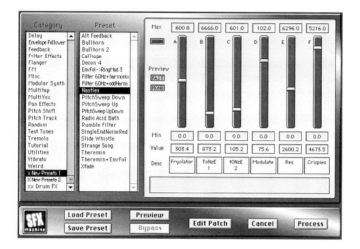

Currently, you can only use plug-ins in Premiere (e.g. Bias Sfx Machine, top diagram) and Audio-Suite (e.g. Digidesign LoFi, bottom diagram) formats in Vst Macintosh in a round-about way via additional host software.

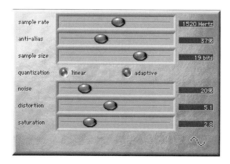

Bias Peak

If you are interested in using this type of ›foreign plug-in‹ in
VST, at this time your only option is run it in another host
app. Although there are numerous audio sequencers for
Macintosh that support AudioSuite, Premiere or even both,
as a Cubase VST user, you are presumably not particularly
thrilled with the prospect of acquiring and working with another sequencer.

Having said this, Bias Peak—audio editing software—is
the ideal supplement to VST Macintosh: It features a Premiere
plug-in interface with enhanced capabilities (an effects rack
that lets you use up to four Premiere effects in realtime to
process stereo files). Version 2.0 will feature an AudioSuite
interface and other handy options such as an integrated CD
burner utility.

Here's how you process audio files via AudioSuite and Premiere effects in Peak or other host software:

1   Record the audio material in VST Macintosh in the usual manner.
    Don't stop the recording immediately after the sequence is in the can,
    instead leave several seconds of silence at the end of the track.

2   Select the file that you want to process (in bold-face type with a trian-
    gle icon) from the AUDIO POOL, not the SEGMENTS (regular typeface
    with speaker icon). Then select the item DUPLICATE FILE from the FILE
    menu.

3   The program will ask you to enter a name for the new file. For the sake
    of simplicity, I recommend you use the original file name plus an ad-
    ditional identifier such as ›E‹—for ›Export‹).

4   Exit VST and start the other host software.

5   In Peak for example, you can import the audio files generated in VST
    directly (FILE ⇨ OPEN) and process them via Premiere or AudioSuite
    effects.

6   The downside is that you can't hear the effects settings in context
    with the other tracks of your VST song. With a bit of effort, you can
    deal with this problem as well: Create different versions with varying
    effects intensities. Save each version under a different name, for in-
    stance ›E1 Name‹ for the driest version (the one with the highest per-
    centage of original signal), ›E9 Name‹ for the wettest version with the

effects signal only (set the effects balance in the plug-in fully to ›Wet‹ or ›Effect‹!).

7 Exit the host software, start VST, import the effects files that you just generated and position these in the ARRANGE window so that they run precisely in sync with the original file. Ensure that all starting points are identical!

8 Now listen to one (and only one, mute all others!) of the generated files in the context of your arrangement. Mute the file and select the next one until you have found the version that delivers the best results for your song.

9 For ›add-on effects‹ such as reverb or delay, it is usually a good idea to play back the original signal in parallel with the thoroughly soaked effects signal (the one we called ›E9‹ in Step 6). You can thus tweak the volumes of the two channels to set the effects balance to taste!

If prior to this operation, you were already working with individual SEGMENTS in the ARRANGEMENT, the procedure for Step 2 is slightly different. Select the SEGMENT that you want to process from the AUDIO POOL instead. Then select the item EXPORT SEGMENT from the local Do menu. If you want to process several SEGMENTS, repeat this step for each one.

3 A Survey of All Plugs

Now that you have the basics down pat, we can get to the fun stuff—shopping for the best plug-ins for the kind of sound bending that you have in mind. The tables in this chapter are a survey of available plug-ins that are compatible with VST. If you like covering all angles and being prepared for every eventuality and decide to load every listed effect to your system, you can spend countless hours scrolling through an effects list several meters long in VST.

Contents of the Tables

The tables are arranged alphabetically by manufacturer name and are pretty much self-explanatory. The following couple of paragraphs should clarify any questions you might have on the various columns.

Platform

Plug-ins that at the time this book went to press were available in a given format are identified with a ✓ in the corresponding column. If a check mark in parentheses (✓) appears in the column, this indicates that the plug-in maker announced that a version for one of the interfaces was in the works, but was as yet unavailable at the time the table was compiled.

CD-ROM Demos

You will find the majority of listed plug-ins as demo versions (for freeware, the fully functional versions) on the included CD-ROM. The symbol ⓞ in a given column of a tables indicates that a version of this plug-in is included on the CD.

If you are interested in a particular plug-in and check out its specs in the table only to find that it is unavailable for your computer platform, be sure to visit the Web site of its maker (see page 240) on the Internet from time to time—the desired version may be forthcoming. You'll find that nowadays virtually all commercial plug-ins will at some point be ported to all leading native formats, so chances are that sooner or later you'll be able to score that plug-in.

CD-ROM Tutorials

Some of the commercial products are unavailable in the form of demo plug-ins, but its makers did program multimedia presentations touting their products. If the CD-ROM includes this type of presentation, a **T** appears in the column.

Details

If you come across a plug-in that sounds like it comes close to what you're looking for and you want to know more about it right away, go to the page indicated in the ›Page‹ column to read a detailed description of the plug-in.

Plug-in prices are ever-changing—it's impossible for list dependable quotes because they may be outdated tomorrow. If you're interested in a given plug-in, contact your retailer to find out the current price.

Note that there are BUNDLES featuring a bunch of plug-ins available. These all-in-one packages are, plug for plug, substantially cheaper than buying each plug-in individually.

Commercial Plugs

First a look at those plugs you'll have to hand over your hard-earned for: If you have a serious jones for one of these plug-ins and your retailer can't help you out, the first place to go for the good word on it is the WWW site of its manufacturer—praised be the Internet.

For many of these plug-ins, Steinberg is the exclusive distributor. This means that you can get them from Steinberg and the company's many licensed dealers. Next to the in-house plugs by Steinberg/Spectral Design, these include the VST plug-ins by Arboretum, Apogee, Prosoniq, Waldorf, SPL as well as Waves Audio Track VST.

Antares

Name	Function	Windows		Mac	
		DirectX	Vst Pc	Vst	Page
Auto Tune Vst	Automatic, editable pitch correction	✓T	—	✓ ⊚	160

Apogee

Name	Function	Windows		Mac	
		DirectX	Vst Pc	Vst	Page
MasterTools	Uv-22 dithering, 3D meter	(✓)	—	(✓)	213

Arboretum

Name	Function	Windows		Mac	
		DirectX	Vst Pc	Vst	Page
Hyperprism	Bundle of diverse effects	✓ ⊚	—	✓ ⊚	202
Ray Gun	Noise reduction	✓ ⊚	—	✓ ⊚	—

Dave Brown

Name	Function	Windows		Mac	
		DirectX	Vst Pc	Vst	Page
ProDelay	Bpm delay	—	✓ ⊚	✓ ⊚	—
ProComp	Compressor/expander	—	✓ ⊚	—	—

Duy

Name	Function	Windows		Mac	
		DirectX	Vst Pc	Vst	Page
Duy Shape	3-band enhancer	—	—	✓ ⊚	—
Max Duy	Level maximizer/limiter	—	—	✓ ⊚	—
Duy Wide	Stereo manipulation	—	—	✓ ⊚	—
DaD Valve	Tube simulation	—	—	✓ ⊚	—
Duy Native Pack	Shape, Max, Wide and Valve in an all-included package	—	—	✓ ⊚	—

Event/Dsp Fx

Name	Function	Windows		Mac	
		DirectX	Vst Pc	Vst	Page
Dsp Fx Virtual Pack	Bundle with all basic effects types (delay, reverb, pitch shifter, flanger, Eq, among others)	✓ ⊚	—	—	—

NeuroSonic

Name	Function	Windows		Mac	Page
		DirectX	Vst Pc	Vst	
GrooveDelay	16-way multi-tap delay	—	✓ ⊚	✓ ⊚	86

Object Productions

Name	Function	Windows		Mac	Page
		DirectX	Vst Pc	Vst	
Vintage Fx Bundle	Bundle with reverb, delay, compressor, limiter, Eqs and diverse modulation effects	(✓)	✓ ⊚	✓ ⊚	211

Opcode

Name	Function	Windows		Mac	Page
		DirectX	Vst Pc	Vst	
fusion:Vocode	5-band vocoder	✓ ⊚	—	—	127
fusion:Vinyl	Vintage vinyl, artificial aging	✓ ⊚	(✓)	(✓)	171
fusion:Filter	Modulatable 3-way effects filter	✓ ⊚	(✓)	(✓)	123
fusion:Vst Fx Bundle	Vinyl, filter and others (chorus, flanger, echo, ring modulator, Rezn8, panner)	(✓)	(✓)	(✓)	—

Prosoniq

Name	Function	Windows		Mac	Page
		DirectX	Vst Pc	Vst	
Voxciter	Combination tool for voice processing (de-esser, compressor, EQ, among others)	—	(✓)	✓ ⊚	153
Roomulator	Room simulation	—	(✓)	✓ ⊚	—
Ambisone	Psychoacoustic 3D-effect	—	(✓)	✓ ⊚	—
Dynasone	Combination tool for mastering (including a multiband compressor)	—	(✓)	✓ ⊚	186
Orange Vocoder	Vocoder with Eq and reverb section	—	(✓)	✓ ⊚	131

Q-Sound

Name	Function	Windows		Mac	Page
		DirectX	Vst Pc	Vst	
Q-Tools	Bundle featuring Qsys Panning, Qxpander Expander, Q123 Mono to Stereo, Qsrc Sample Rate Converter	✓	—	—	—

R. S. Plieger

Name	Function	Windows DirectX	VST Pc	Mac VST	Page
VST Compressor	Compressor/limiter	—	✓ ◉	—	—

Sipab

Name	Function	Windows DirectX	VST Pc	Mac VST	Page
QuickVerb	Room simulation	✓T	—	—	—
MultiVerb	Room simulation	✓ ◉ T	—	—	—
LawnMover	4-band parametric EQ	✓ T	—	—	—

Sonic Foundry

Name	Function	Windows DirectX	VST Pc	Mac VST	Page
Noise Reduction	De-noiser/de-clicker, vinyl restoration	✓ ◉	—	—	—
Acoustic Mirror	Room analysis/simulation	✓ ◉	—	—	—
XFX 1 Plug-in Pack	Bundle with basic effects (reverb, time/pitch-shift, delay, chorus, among others)	✓ ◉	—	—	—
XFX 2 Plug-in Pack	Bundle with mastering effects (multiband dynamics, diverse EQs, among others)	✓ ◉	—	—	—
XFX 3 Plug-in Pack	Bundle with sound design effects (amplitude modulation, gapper/snipper, flange/wah-wah, vibrato, distortion, enhancer)	✓ ◉	—	—	—

SPL

Name	Function	Windows DirectX	VST Pc	Mac VST	Page
De-Esser	De-esser	✓ T	—	✓ T	147

Steinberg/Spectral Design

Name	Function	Windows DirectX	VST Pc	Mac VST	Page
DeClicker	Restoration/Click removal	✓	—	✓ ◉	183
DeNoiser	Noise removal	✓ T	—	✓ ◉ T	180
Loudness Maximizer	Level/loudness maximization	✓	—	✓ ◉	—
Magneto	Analog tape saturation simulation	✓	—	✓ ◉	169

Steinberg/Spectral Design (cont.)

Name	Function	Windows DirectX	Windows VST Pc	Mac VST	Page
Red Valve-It	Virtual guitar stack featuring tube amp and cabinets	—	—	✓ ◉	—
Spectralizer	Enhancer/exciter	✓	—	✓	108
Free-D	3-D positioning (over-/behind head orientation)	—	—	✓	—
Free Filter	Filter	✓ **T**	—	✓ **T**	103
Q-Metric	High-quality 7-band EQ	✓ **T**	✓	✓ **T**	90
QuadraFuzz	Fuzz with four separate filter/distortion bands	(✓)	(✓)	(✓)	—
MultiComp	Multiband compressor with four bands	(✓)	(✓)	(✓)	—
Ultravox	Pitch/formant shifter	—	✓	✓	165

Synchromesh

Name	Function	Windows DirectX	Windows VST Pc	Mac VST	Page
EQ64	Stereo parametric EQ with 64 bands	—	✓	✓	—
TriComp	3-band dynamics processor	—	✓	✓	—

Tc Works

Name	Function	Windows DirectX	Windows VST Pc	Mac VST	Page
Native Reverb	Room simulation	✓ ◉	✓ ◉	✓ ◉	79
Native EQ	28-band graphic EQ and	✓ ◉	✓ ◉	—	96
	10-band parametric EQ	—	✓ ◉	—	95
Native DeX	Compressor/de-esser combination	(✓)	(✓)	—	215
Native Essentials	Bundle featuring basic EQ, compressor and reverb (not equivalent to the other Tc native plug-ins)	✓ ◉	—	—	209
Native Bundle	Native Reverb, EQ and DeX in a bundle	(✓)	(✓)	—	208

Thomas Rehaag

Name	Function	Windows DirectX	Windows VST Pc	Mac VST	Page
AUM	Low-pass sweep filter	—	✓ ◉	—	—
PSI	Phase Shift Iterator (phaser/flanger)	—	✓ ◉	—	—

Timeworks

Name	Function	Windows		Mac	
		DirectX	Vst Pc	Vst	Page
Reverb 480L	Room simulation	✓ ⊚	—	—	—
Delay 6022	Stereo delay	✓ ⊚	—	—	—
Phazer Model 88	Phaser	✓ ⊚	—	—	—
Mastering Eq	Equalizer	✓ ⊚	—	—	—

Vincent Burel

Name	Function	Windows		Mac	
		DirectX	Vst Pc	Vst	Page
Aphro-V1	High-end reverb	(✓)	—	—	—

Waldorf

Name	Function	Windows		Mac	
		DirectX	Vst Pc	Vst	Page
D-Pole	MicroWave II synthesizer's modulatable synthesis filter	—	✓ ⊚	✓ ⊚	118

Waves

Name	Function	Windows		Mac	
		DirectX	Vst Pc	Vst	Page
TrueVerb	Room simulation	✓ ⊚ *	—	✓ ⊚ *	74
Q10	Parametric Eq with a max. of ten stereo bands	✓ ⊚ *	—	✓ ⊚ *	98
C1	Different combinations of compressor/ expander/gate	✓ ⊚ *	—	✓ ⊚ *	135
L1	Loudness maximizer/limiter	✓ ⊚ *	—	✓ ⊚ *	190
S1	Stereo manipulation	✓ ⊚ *	—	✓ ⊚ *	176
Idr	Dithering	✓ ⊚ *	—	✓ ⊚ *	192
Audio Track Vst	4-band Eq/compressor/ expander/gate combination	✓ ⊚	—	✓ ⊚	157
MaxxBass	Psychoacoustic bass maximizer	✓ ⊚	—	✓ ⊚	113
DeEsser	De-esser	✓ ⊚	—	✓ ⊚	150
Paz	Analyzer (frequency/energy, correlation, level)	—	—	✓ ⊚	196
Renaissance Compressor	Tube compressor	✓ ⊚	—	✓ ⊚	142

Waves (cont.)

Name	Function	Windows DirectX	Windows Vst Pc	Mac Vst	Page
Renaissance EQ	Vintage equalizer	✓ ⊛	—	✓	—
Native Power Pack (Npp)	Bundle featuring TrueVerb, Q10, C1, L1, S1, Idr (plus Track Pac lite—file compression)	✓ ⊛	—	✓ ⊛	206
EasyWaves	Bundle featuring basic reverb, compressor and EQ	✓ ⊛	—	✓	—

* Component part of Npp (see page 206)

Internal Vst Plug-ins

For the record, we should of course take a look at the plug-ins that ship with Vst. Check out the respective column to see where you can find more info on a given effect, or simply compare platforms to see what you as Macintosh user have that Pc users don't and vice versa. Feel free to gloat or pout as appropriate.

Steinberg

Name	Function	Windows DirectX	Windows Vst Pc	Mac Vst	Wizoo Guide Vst Win Page	Wizoo Guide Vst Mac Page
WunderVerb3	Room simulation	—	✓	✓	100	127
Electro Fuzz	Distortion	—	✓	✓	96	124
Grungelizer	Lo-fi/vintage	—	✓	—	97	—
Scopion	Oscilloscope	—	✓	✓	101	129
ESpacial	Room simulation	—	✓	✓	95	123
Stereo Echo	Delay	—	✓	✓	98	125
Choirus	Chorus	—	✓	✓	94	122
Choirus 2	Chorus	—	—	✓	—	122
AutoPan	Stereo panning	—	✓	✓	93	121
Stereo Wizard	Stereo spread	—	✓	✓	102	130

Steinberg/Spectral Design

| Name | Function | Windows | | Mac | WIZOO Guide | |
		DirectX	VST Pc	VST	VST Win Page	VST Mac Page
Tun-A	Chromatic tuner	—	—	✓	—	128
Externalizer	Pyschoacoustic 3-D simulation for headphones mixes	—	—	✓	—	131

Freeware Plug-ins

Here's a truly philanthropic innovation: free plug-ins. It's a bit hard to stay on top of what's hip in terms of freeware plug-ins; it seems new stuff is offered on a daily basis. If you have Internet access, you should occasionally update your arsenal. A good place to get started is the site index at Cubase Webring (see page 239).

▶ You can only download Steinberg freeware plug-ins personally. In other words, you have to go to the Steinberg Web site and proffer your email address in return for the opportunity to download. Also, offers are limited, available only for a given amount of time. For example, the TranceMitter listed here is already no longer available from the Steinberg site. It's a good idea to check in regularly and grab what's available as soon as it's offered, 'cause it could be gone tomorrow.

Aldo Trianti

| Name | Function | Windows | | Mac | Page |
		DirectX	VST Pc	VST	
xVerb	Room simulation	—	✓ ⊚	—	221
xChorus	Four-voice chorus	—	✓ ⊚	—	—
xFaser Lite	Phaser (limited parameters)	—	✓ ⊚	—	—
xlm Delay	Delay with Lp filter	—	✓ ⊚	—	—
Noise Gate	Noise gate with one frequency band	—	✓ ⊚	—	—
Multiband Noise Gate	Noise Gate with three frequency bands	—	✓ ⊚	—	—

Arboretum

Name	Function	Windows DirectX	VST Pc	Mac VST	Page
Free Hyper-prism VST	Three plugs from Hyperprism VST as fully functional versions (High Pass, Low Pass, Ring Modulator)	—	✓ ⊚	✓ ⊚	202

Bo Johansen

Name	Function	Windows DirectX	VST Pc	Mac VST	Page
BJ Flanger	Flanger/chorus	—	✓ ⊚	—	228
BJ Lo-fi	Lo-fi/retro plug-in for noise, distortion etc.	—	✓ ⊚	—	—
BJ Overdrive	Distortion	—	✓ ⊚	—	—
BJ RingModula-tor	You guessed it, a ring modulator	—	✓ ⊚	—	—
BJ Tremolo	Tremolo with six LFO waveforms and auto-pan-ning option	—	✓ ⊚	—	—
BJ Wavechanger	Analog synth effect (replaces audio with simple analog waveforms)	—	✓ ⊚	—	—

Dave Brown

Name	Function	Windows DirectX	VST Pc	Mac VST	Page
dB Tempo Delay	BPM delay	✓ ⊚	✓ ⊚	✓ ⊚	223
dB Sweep Delay	Modulatable BPM delay	—	✓ ⊚	✓ ⊚	223
dB Tremelo	Tremolo modulation with auto-panning	—	✓ ⊚	✓ ⊚	—
dB Compressor	Compressor	—	✓ ⊚	—	—

Digilogue

Name	Function	Windows DirectX	VST Pc	Mac VST	Page
BluePhaser	Eight-voice phaser	✓ ⊚	✓ ⊚	—	232
BlueFlanger	Flanger	✓ ⊚	✓ ⊚	—	232
BlueChorus	Four-voice chorus	✓ ⊚	✓ ⊚	—	232
BlueDelay	Tempo delay	✓ ⊚	✓ ⊚	—	233
BlueMultiTap	Multi-tap tempo delay	✓ ⊚	✓ ⊚	—	233
BlueParamEQ	4-band parametric EQ	✓ ⊚	✓ ⊚	—	233

Digilogue (cont.)

Name	Function	Windows		Mac	
		DirectX	Vst Pc	Vst	Page
BlueFilter	Synth filter with modulation	✓ (●)	✓ (●)	—	234
BlueCompressor	Compressor	✓ (●)	✓ (●)	—	234
BlueReverb	Room simulation	✓ (●)	✓ (●)	—	234
BlueStereo	Pseudo stereo	✓ (●)	✓ (●)	—	234
BlueGate	Noise gate with ADSR envelope	✓ (●)	✓ (●)	—	234

Digital Elements

Name	Function	Windows		Mac	
		DirectX	Vst Pc	Vst	Page
Compressor	Actually, an upward expander	—	✓ (●)	—	—

Div/Zero

Name	Function	Windows		Mac	
		DirectX	Vst Pc	Vst	Page
RingModulator	Yes, a ring modulator	—	✓ (●)	✓ (●)	—

Fraser Stuart

Name	Function	Windows		Mac	
		DirectX	Vst Pc	Vst	Page
F_Comp	Compressor (mono and stereo version)	—	✓ (●)	✓ (●)	—
F_EqShelf	Mono Shelf EQ (mono and stereo version)	—	✓ (●)	✓ (●)	—
F_Tube	Mono tube overdrive (mono and stereo version)	—	✓ (●)	✓ (●)	—
F_S_EqFilter	Stereo high-/low-pass filter	—	✓ (●)	✓ (●)	—
F_S_LineT	Stereo line trim module	—	✓ (●)	✓ (●)	—
F_S_Phase	Stereo phase switch	—	✓ (●)	✓ (●)	—

J. Schmitt

Name	Function	Windows		Mac	
		DirectX	Vst Pc	Vst	Page
Js 6 Equalizer	6-band equalizer	—	✓ (●)	—	—
Js Band Cut	Band-pass filter	—	✓ (●)	—	—
Js Compresseur	Compressor	—	✓ (●)	—	—
Js Disto	Distortion	—	✓ (●)	—	—

J. Schmitt (cont.)

Name	Function	Windows DirectX	VST Pc	Mac VST	Page
Js Equalizer	3-band equalizer	—	✓ ⊚	—	—
Js Humanizer	Modulating resonance filter with vocal formants (sounds like a human voice)	—	✓ ⊚	—	—
Js Limiteur	Limiter	—	✓ ⊚	—	—
Js Magneto	›Copy‹ of the Steinberg/Spectral Design plug-in Magneto	—	✓ ⊚	—	—
Js Mini-Sample	Sampler/buffer	—	✓ ⊚	—	—
Js Noise Attenu	Noise gate	—	✓ ⊚	—	—
Js Noise Filtre	Noise suppression	—	✓ ⊚	—	—
Js Oscil resonne 2	Synthis filter with Lfo	—	✓ ⊚	—	—
Js Oscil resonne 3	See above (different fundamental sound)	—	✓ ⊚	—	—
Js PanDelay	Panning delay	—	✓ ⊚	—	—
Js Resonnateur	Synthesis filter sans modulation	—	✓ ⊚	—	—
Js Vibrato	Vibrato	—	✓ ⊚	—	—

Living Memory

Name	Function	Windows DirectX	VST Pc	Mac VST	Page
Flanger	Flanger (on Steinberg's Plug-in Zone Cd)	—	—	✓	—
Resonant Filter	Resonance capable Filter (on Steinberg's Plug-in Zone Cd)	—	—	✓	—
Reverb	Room simulation (on Steinberg's Plug-in Zone Cd)	—	—	✓	—
Spatializer	Stereo manipulation (on Steinberg's Plug-in Zone Cd)	—	—	✓	—

Maxim

Name	Function	Windows DirectX	VST Pc	Mac VST	Page
Overdrive	Tube-like distortion (featured in mda Pack 1)	—	✓ ⊚	✓ ⊚	—
RoundPan	Panning with 3D effect (featured in mda Pack 1)	—	✓ ⊚	✓ ⊚	—
RingMod	Ring modulation with sine oscillator (featured in mda Pack 1)	—	✓ ⊚	✓ ⊚	—

Maxim (cont.)

Name	Function	Windows DirectX	Windows VST Pc	Mac VST	Page
ThruZero	Flanger (featured in mda Pack 1)	—	✓ ⊛	✓ ⊛	—
Limiter	Brickwall limiter (featured in mda Pack 2)	—	✓ ⊛	✓ ⊛	—
Stereo	Mono to stereo (featured in mda Pack 2)	—	✓ ⊛	✓ ⊛	—
Re-Psycho	Effects pitch shifter (featured in mda Pack 2)	—	✓ ⊛	✓ ⊛	—
SubSynth	Sub-bass generator (featured in mda Pack 2)	—	✓ ⊛	✓ ⊛	—
Bandisto	Harsh multi-band distortion (featured in mda Pack 3)	—	✓ ⊛	✓	—
Beat Box	Replaces waveforms with internal samples (with recording option) (featured in mda Pack 3)	—	✓ ⊛	✓	—
Combo	Speaker simulation (featured in mda Pack 3)	—	✓ ⊛	✓	—
Degrade	Lo-fi effect (featured in mda Pack 3)	—	✓ ⊛	✓	—
Dynamics	Compressor/limiter/gate combination (featured in mda Pack 3)	—	✓ ⊛	✓	—
MultiBand	3-band compressor (featured in mda Pack 4)	—	✓ ⊛	✓	—
RezFilter	Synth filter (similar to Steinberg Trancemitter) (featured in mda Pack 4)	—	✓ ⊛	✓	—
Shepard	Shepard test tone generator (featured in mda Pack 4)	—	✓ ⊛	✓	—
TestTone	Test tone generator with sine and white/pink noise, among others (featured in mda Pack 4)	—	✓ ⊛	✓	—
Tracker	Pitch modulation with Lfo (featured in mda Pack 4)	—	✓ ⊛	✓	—

Prosoniq

Name	Function	Windows DirectX	Windows VST Pc	Mac VST	Page
North Pole	Resonance filter	—	✓ ⊛	✓ ⊛	230

Steinberg

Name	Function	Windows DirectX	Windows VST Pc	Mac VST	Page
TranceMitter	Resonance-capable filter	—	✓	—	—
Chopper	Segment cutter/rearrangement	—	✓	—	—

Synchromesh

| Name | Function | Windows | | Mac | |
		DirectX	VST Pc	VST	Page
KwikKomp2	Compressor/limiter	—	✓ ⊚	✓ ⊚	—

Thomas Rehaag

| Name | Function | Windows | | Mac | |
		DirectX	VST Pc	VST	Page
Spice 1	Distortion	—	✓ ⊚	—	—
Spice 2	Distortion (different sound)	—	✓ ⊚	—	—
Vibrator	Frequency vibrato	—	✓ ⊚	—	—

Vellocet

| Name | Function | Windows | | Mac | |
		DirectX	VST Pc	VST	Page
VFilterNode	Resonance-capable filter	—	✓ ⊚	✓ ⊚	—
VPingPong	Delay	—	✓ ⊚	✓ ⊚	—
VFlanger	Flanger	—	✓ ⊚	✓ ⊚	—
VNoPhones	External localization for headphones mixing	—	✓ ⊚	✓ ⊚	—
VReOrder	Cutting/re-organization	—	✓ ⊚	✓ ⊚	225
VNoiseGate	Noise gate	—	✓ ⊚	✓ ⊚	—

Vincent Burel

| Name | Function | Windows | | Mac | |
		DirectX	VST Pc	VST	Page
Stereoizer	Mono to stereo	—	✓ ⊚	—	—
D Limiter	Limiter	—	✓ ⊚	—	—
Karakao	Phase manipulation, lowering the level of solo/vocal sounds in backing tracks	—	✓ ⊚	—	—
Ping Pong Disto	Filter/cross-delay	—	✓ ⊚	—	—
Megatrancer	Synthesis filter	—	✓ ⊚	—	—

The Seek-and-Ye-Shall-Plug-in Finder

In this section, you'll find a survey of plug-ins ordered alphabetically by effects type. It is a good place to get started if you're in the market for a specific effect and want to find out which plug-ins will do the job.

An Overview of Effects Types

Category	Effects
Room simulation	Reverb, early reflections
Delay	BPM, ping-pong, cross-delay
EQ	Parametric and graphic filters, voicing sections for channel processing and mastering
Enhancer	Psychoacoustic filters, enhancers, exciters, bass maximizers and optimizes
Synth filters	Resonance and synth filters, usually with modulation options
Modulation	Flangers, phasers, ring modulators, vocoders
Sound design	Wacky effects: Chop up, reorganize, swap, and bend audio signals (beyond recognition, if you so desire)
Dynamics	Compressor, expanders, de-essers, gates, limiters
Pitch	Pitch modulation and correction, pitch shifters
Vintage	Lo-fi effects, virtual analog stuff such as tape saturation, fuzz, distortion, speaker simulation
Stereo	Stereo spread manipulation, 3-D sound, auto-panners, phase inversion
Restoration	De-noiser, noise gates, de-clickers, de-cracklers
Dithering	Dithering tools for mastering
Combination	Universal effects combinations in a single plug-in
Display	Analyzers, level meters, oscilloscopes, tuners
Tool	Small but helpful audio utilities, signal generators
Commercial bundles	Plug-in packages for all types of applications

An Overview of All Plug-ins by Effects Type

Here's a brief explanation of symbols and abbreviations used in this table:

⊚—included as a demo or fully functional version on the Cᴅ-Rᴏᴍ,

T—presentation on Cᴅ-Rᴏᴍ
Commerc.—commercials plug-in
Internal—internal Vsᴛ plug-in
Free/share—freeware or shareware plug-in

Room Simulation

Manufacturer	Name	Status	Windows DirectX	Windows Vsᴛ Pc	Mac Vsᴛ	Page
Aldo Trianti	xVerb	Free/share	—	✓ ⊚	—	221
Digilogue	BlueReverb	Free/share	✓ ⊚	✓ ⊚	—	234
Living Memory	Reverb	Free/share	—	—	✓	—
Prosoniq	Roomulator	Commerc.	—	(✓)	✓ ⊚	—
Sipab	QuickVerb	Commerc.	✓T	—	—	—
Sipab	MultiVerb	Commerc.	✓ ⊚ T	—	—	—
Sonic Foundry	Acoustic Mirror	Commerc.	✓ ⊚	—	—	—
Steinberg	WunderVerb3	Internal	—	✓	✓	—
Steinberg	ESpacial	Internal	—	✓	✓	—
Tc Works	Native Reverb	Commerc.	✓ ⊚	✓ ⊚	✓ ⊚	79
Timeworks	Reverb 480L	Commerc.	✓ ⊚	—	—	—
Vincent Burel	Aᴘʜʀᴏ-V1	Commerc.	(✓)	—	—	—
Waves	TrueVerb	Commerc.	✓ ⊚ (Nᴘᴘ)	—	✓ ⊚ (Nᴘᴘ)	74

Delay

Manufacturer	Name	Status	Windows DirectX	Windows Vsᴛ Pc	Mac Vsᴛ	Page
Aldo Trianti	xlm Delay	Free/share	—	✓ ⊚	—	—
Dave Brown	dB Tempo Delay	Free/share	✓ ⊚	✓ ⊚	✓ ⊚	223
Dave Brown	dB Sweep Delay	Free/share	—	✓ ⊚	✓ ⊚	223
Dave Brown	ProDelay	Commerc.	—	✓ ⊚	✓ ⊚	—

Delay (cont.)

Manufacturer	Name	Status	Windows DirectX	Windows VST Pc	Mac Vst	Page
Digilogue	BlueDelay	Free/share	✓ ⊚	✓ ⊚	—	233
Digilogue	BlueMultiTap	Free/share	✓ ⊚	✓ ⊚	—	233
J.Schmitt	Js PanDelay	Free/share	—	✓ ⊚	—	—
NeuroSonic	GrooveDelay	Commerc.	—	✓ ⊚	✓ ⊚	86
Steinberg	Stereo Echo	Internal	—	✓	✓	—
Timeworks	Delay 6022	Commerc.	✓ ⊚	—	—	—
Vellocet	VPingPong	Free/share	—	✓ ⊚	✓ ⊚	—

EQ

Manufacturer	Name	Status	Windows DirectX	Windows VST Pc	Mac Vst	Page
Apogee	MasterTools	Commerc.	(✓)	—	(✓)	213
Digilogue	BlueParamEQ	Free/share	✓ ⊚	✓ ⊚	—	233
Fraser Stuart	F_EqShelf	Free/share	—	✓ ⊚	✓ ⊚	—
Fraser Stuart	F_S_EqFilter	Free/share	—	✓ ⊚	✓ ⊚	—
J.Schmitt	Js 6 Equalizer	Free/share	—	✓ ⊚	—	—
J.Schmitt	Js Band Cut	Free/share	—	✓ ⊚	—	—
J.Schmitt	Js Equalizer	Free/share	—	✓ ⊚	—	—
Sipab	LawnMover	Commerc.	✓ T	—	—	—
Steinberg/Spectral Design	Free Filter	Commerc.	✓ T	—	✓ T	103
Steinberg/Spectral Design	Q-Metric	Commerc.	✓ T	✓	✓ T	90
Synchromesh	EQ64	Commerc.	—	✓	✓	—
Tc Works	Native EQ: graphic EQ	Commerc.	✓ ⊚	✓ ⊚	—	96
	Native EQ: parametric EQ		—	✓ ⊚	—	95
Timeworks	Mastering EQ	Commerc.	✓ ⊚	—	—	—
Waves	Q10	Commerc.	✓ ⊚ (Npp)	—	✓ ⊚ (Npp)	98
Waves	Renaissance EQ	Commerc.	✓ ⊚	—	✓	—

Enhancer

| Manufacturer | Name | Status | Windows | | Mac | Page |
			DirectX	Vst Pc	Vst	
Duy	Duy Shape	Commerc.	—	—	✓ ⊚	—
Maxim	SubSynth	Free/share	—	✓ ⊚	✓ ⊚	—
Steinberg/ Spectral Design	Spectralizer	Commerc.	✓	—	✓	108
Waves	MaxxBass	Commerc.	✓ ⊚	—	✓ ⊚	113

Synth Filters

| Manufacturer | Name | Status | Windows | | Mac | Page |
			DirectX	Vst Pc	Vst	
Digilogue	BlueFilter	Free/share	✓ ⊚	✓ ⊚	—	234
J.Schmitt	Js Humanizer	Free/share	—	✓ ⊚	—	—
J.Schmitt	Js Oscil resonne 2	Free/share	—	✓ ⊚	—	—
J.Schmitt	Js Oscil resonne 3	Free/share	—	✓ ⊚	—	—
J.Schmitt	Js Resonnateur	Free/share	—	✓ ⊚	—	—
Living Memory	Resonant Filter	Free/share	—	—	✓	—
Maxim	RezFilter	Free/share	—	✓ ⊚	✓	—
Opcode	fusion:Filter	Commerc.	✓ ⊚	(✓)	(✓)	123
Prosoniq	North Pole	Free/share	—	✓ ⊚	✓ ⊚	230
Steinberg	TranceMitter	Free/share	—	✓	—	—
Thomas Rehaag	Aum	Commerc.	—	✓ ⊚	—	—
Vellocet	VFilterNode	Free/share	—	✓ ⊚	✓ ⊚	—
Vincent Burel	Megatrancer	Free/share	—	✓ ⊚	—	—
Waldorf	D-Pole	Commerc.	—	✓ ⊚	✓ ⊚	118

Modulation

| Manufacturer | Name | Status | Windows | | Mac | Page |
			DirectX	Vst Pc	Vst	
Aldo Trianti	xChorus	Free/share	—	✓ ⊚	—	—
Aldo Trianti	xFaser Lite	Free/share	—	✓ ⊚	—	—
Bo Johansen	Bj Flanger	Free/share	—	✓ ⊚	—	228
Bo Johansen	Bj RingModulator	Free/share	—	✓ ⊚	—	—
Bo Johansen	Bj Tremolo	Free/share	—	✓ ⊚	—	—

Modulation (cont.)

Manufacturer	Name	Status	Windows DirectX	Windows Vst Pc	Mac Vst	Page
Dave Brown	dB Tremelo	Free/share	—	✓	✓	—
Digilogue	BluePhaser	Free/share	✓	✓	—	232
Digilogue	BlueFlanger	Free/share	✓	✓	—	232
Digilogue	BlueChorus	Free/share	✓	✓	—	232
Div/Zero	Ring modulator	Free/share	—	✓	✓	—
J.Schmitt	Js Vibrato	Free/share	—	✓	—	—
Living Memory	Flanger	Free/share	—	—	✓	—
Maxim	RingMod	Free/share	—	✓	✓	—
Maxim	ThruZero	Free/share	—	✓	✓	—
Opcode	fusion:Vocode	Commerc.	✓	—	—	127
Prosoniq	Orange Vocoder	Commerc.	—	(✓)	✓	131
Steinberg	Choirus	Internal	—	✓	✓	—
Steinberg	Choirus 2	Internal	—	—	✓	—
Thomas Rehaag	Psi	Commerc.	—	✓	—	—
Thomas Rehaag	Vibrator	Free/share	—	✓	—	—
Timeworks	Phazer Model 88	Commerc.	✓	—	—	—
Vellocet	VFlanger	Free/share	—	✓	✓	—

Sound Design

Manufacturer	Name	Status	Windows DirectX	Windows Vst Pc	Mac Vst	Page
Bo Johansen	BJ Wavechanger	Free/share	—	✓	—	—
Maxim	Re-Psycho	Free/share	—	✓	✓	—
Maxim	Beat Box	Free/share	—	✓	✓	—
Steinberg	Chopper	Free/share	—	✓	—	—
Vellocet	VReOrder	Free/share	—	✓	✓	225

Dynamics

Manufacturer	Name	Status	Windows		Mac	Page
			DirectX	Vst Pc	Vst	
Dave Brown	dB Compressor	Free/share	—	✓ ⊛	—	—
Dave Brown	ProComp	Commerc.	—	✓ ⊛	—	—
Digilogue	BlueCompressor	Free/share	✓ ⊛	✓ ⊛	—	234
Digital Elements	Compressor	Free/share	—	✓ ⊛	—	—
Duy	Max Duy	Commerc.	—	—	✓ ⊛	—
Fraser Stuart	F_Comp	Free/share	—	✓ ⊛	✓ ⊛	—
J.Schmitt	Js Compresseur	Free/share	—	✓ ⊛	—	—
J.Schmitt	Js Limiteur	Free/share	—	✓ ⊛	—	—
Maxim	Limiter	Free/share	—	✓ ⊛	✓ ⊛	—
Maxim	Dynamics	Free/share	—	✓ ⊛	✓	—
Maxim	MultiBand	Free/share	—	✓ ⊛	✓	—
R. S. Plieger	Vst Compressor	Commerc.	—	✓ ⊛	—	—
Spl	De-Esser	Commerc.	✓ T	—	✓ T	147
Steinberg/ Spectral Design	Loudness Maximizer	Commerc.	✓	—	✓ ⊛	—
Steinberg/ Spectral Design	MultiComp	Commerc.	(✓)	(✓)	(✓)	217
Synchromesh	KwikKomp2	Free/share	—	✓ ⊛	✓ ⊛	—
Synchromesh	TriComp	Free/share	—	✓	✓	—
Tc Works	Native DeX	Commerc.	(✓)	(✓)	—	215
Vincent Burel	D Limiter	Free/share	—	✓ ⊛	—	—
Waves	C1	Commerc.	✓ ⊛ (Npp)	—	✓ ⊛ (Npp)	135
Waves	L1	Commerc.	✓ ⊛ (Npp)	—	✓ ⊛ (Npp)	190
Waves	DeEsser	Commerc.	✓ ⊛	—	✓ ⊛	150
Waves	Renaissance Compressor	Commerc.	✓ ⊛	—	✓ ⊛	142

Pitch

Manufacturer	Name	Status	Windows		Mac	Page
			DirectX	Vst Pc	Vst	
Antares	Auto Tune Vst	Commerc.	✓T	—	✓ ⊚	160
Maxim	Tracker	Free/share	—	✓ ⊚	✓	—
Steinberg/ Spectral Design	Ultravox	Commerc.	—	✓	✓	165

Vintage

Manufacturer	Name	Status	Windows		Mac	Page
			DirectX	Vst Pc	Vst	
Bo Johansen	Bj lo-fi	Free/share	—	✓ ⊚	—	—
Bo Johansen	Bj Overdrive	Free/share	—	✓ ⊚	—	—
Duy	DaD Valve	Commerc.	—	—	✓ ⊚	—
Fraser Stuart	F_Tube	Free/share	—	✓ ⊚	✓ ⊚	—
J.Schmitt	Js Disto	Free/share	—	✓ ⊚	—	—
J.Schmitt	Js Magneto	Free/share	—	✓ ⊚	—	—
Maxim	Overdrive	Free/share	—	✓ ⊚	✓ ⊚	—
Maxim	Bandisto	Free/share	—	✓ ⊚	✓	—
Maxim	Combo	Free/share	—	✓ ⊚	✓	—
Maxim	Degrade	Free/share	—	✓ ⊚	✓	—
Opcode	fusion:Vinyl	Commerc.	✓ ⊚	(✓)	(✓)	171
Steinberg	Electro Fuzz	Internal	—	✓	✓	—
Steinberg	Grungelizer	Internal	—	✓	—	—
Steinberg/ Spectral Design	Magneto	Commerc.	✓	—	✓ ⊚	169
Steinberg/ Spectral Design	Red Valve-It	Commerc.	—	—	✓ ⊚	—
Steinberg/ Spectral Design	QuadraFuzz	Commerc.	(✓)	(✓)	(✓)	218
Thomas Rehaag	Spice 1	Free/share	—	✓ ⊚	—	—
Thomas Rehaag	Spice 2	Free/share	—	✓ ⊚	—	—
Vincent Burel	Ping Pong Disto	Free/share	—	✓ ⊚	—	—

Stereo

Manufacturer	Name	Status	Windows		Mac	
			DirectX	Vst Pc	Vst	Page
Digilogue	BlueStereo	Free/share	✓⊕	✓⊕	—	234
Duy	Duy Wide	Commerc.	—	—	✓⊕	—
Fraser Stuart	F_S_Phase	Free/share	—	✓⊕	✓⊕	—
Living Memory	Spatializer	Free/share	—	—	✓	—
Maxim	RoundPan	Free/share	—	✓⊕	✓⊕	—
Maxim	Stereo	Free/share	—	✓⊕	✓⊕	—
Prosoniq	Ambisone	Commerc.	—	(✓)	✓⊕	—
Q-Sound	Q-Tools	Commerc.	✓	—	—	—
Steinberg	AutoPan	Internal	—	✓	✓	—
Steinberg	Stereo Wizard	Internal	—	✓	✓	—
Steinberg/Spectral Design	Externalizer	Internal	—	—	✓	—
Steinberg/Spectral Design	Free-D	Commerc.	—	—	✓	—
Vellocet	VNoPhones	Free/share	—	✓⊕	✓⊕	—
Vincent Burel	Stereoizer	Free/share	—	✓⊕	—	—
Vincent Burel	Karakao	Free/share	—	✓⊕	—	—
Waves	S1	Commerc.	✓⊕ (Npp)	—	✓⊕ (Npp)	176

Restoration

Manufacturer	Name	Status	Windows		Mac	
			DirectX	Vst Pc	Vst	Page
Aldo Trianti	Noise Gate	Free/share	—	✓⊕	—	—
Aldo Trianti	Multiband Noise Gate	Free/share	—	✓⊕	—	—
Arboretum	Ray Gun	Commerc.	✓⊕	—	✓⊕	—
Arboretum	Noise Reduction	Commerc.	✓⊕	—	—	—
Digilogue	BlueGate	Free/share	✓⊕	✓⊕	—	234
J.Schmitt	Js Noise Attenu	Free/share	—	✓⊕	—	—
J.Schmitt	Js Noise Filtre	Free/share	—	✓⊕	—	—

Restoration (cont.)

Manufacturer	Name	Status	Windows DirectX	Windows Vst Pc	Mac Vst	Page
Steinberg/ Spectral Design	DeClicker	Commerc.	✓	—	✓ ⓔ	183
Steinberg/ Spectral Design	DeNoiser	Commerc.	✓ **T**	—	✓ ⓔ **T**	180
Vellocet	VNoiseGate	Free/share	—	✓ ⓔ	✓ ⓔ	—

Dithering

Manufacturer	Name	Status	Windows DirectX	Windows Vst Pc	Mac Vst	Page
Waves	IDR	Commerc.	✓ ⓔ (NPP)	—	✓ ⓔ (NPP)	192

Combination

Manufacturer	Name	Status	Windows DirectX	Windows Vst Pc	Mac Vst	Page
Prosoniq	Voxciter	Commerc.	—	(✓)	✓ ⓔ	153
Prosoniq	Dynasone	Commerc.	—	(✓)	✓ ⓔ	186
Waves	Audio Track Vst	Commerc.	✓ ⓔ	—	✓ ⓔ	157

Display

Manufacturer	Name	Status	Windows DirectX	Windows Vst Pc	Mac Vst	Page
Steinberg	Scopion	Internal	—	✓	✓	—
Steinberg/ Spectral Design	Tun-A	Internal	—	—	✓	—
Waves	Paz	Commerc.	—	—	✓ ⓔ	196

Tool

Manufacturer	Name	Status	Windows DirectX	Windows Vst Pc	Mac Vst	Page
Fraser Stuart	F_S_LineT	Free/share	—	✓ ⓔ	✓ ⓔ	—
J.Schmitt	Js Mini-Sample	Free/share	—	✓ ⓔ	—	—
Maxim	Shepard	Free/share	—	✓ ⓔ	✓	—
Maxim	TestTone	Free/share	—	✓ ⓔ	✓	—

Commercial Bundles

Manufacturer	Name	Status	Windows		Mac	Page
			DirectX	Vst Pc	Vst	
Arboretum	Hyperprism	Commerc.	✓ ⊛	—	✓ ⊛	202
Duy	Duy Native Pack	Commerc.	—	—	✓ ⊛	—
Event/Dsp Fx	Dsp Fx Virtual Pack	Commerc.	✓ ⊛	—	—	—
Object Productions	Vintage Fx Bundle	Commerc.	(✓)	✓ ⊛	✓ ⊛	211
Opcode	fusion:Vst Fx Bundle	Commerc.	(✓)	(✓)	(✓)	—
Sonic Foundry	Xfx 1, Plug-in Pack	Commerc.	✓ ⊛	—	—	—
Sonic Foundry	Xfx 2, Plug-in-Pack	Commerc.	✓ ⊛	—	—	—
Sonic Foundry	Xfx 3, Plug-in-Pack	Commerc.	✓ ⊛	—	—	—
Tc Works	Native Essentials	Commerc.	✓ ⊛	—	—	209
Tc Works	Native Bundle	Commerc.	(✓)	(✓)	—	208
Waves	Native Power Pack (Npp)	Commerc.	✓ ⊛	—	✓ ⊛	206
Waves	EasyWaves	Commerc.	✓ ⊛	—	✓	—

4 The Best Commercial Plug-ins

In the following chapter, we'll take a detailed look at the commercial plug-ins which—in my humble opinion—particularly merit recommendation or at least honorable mention. This collection of—in my book—›hip‹ programs was selected so that at least one plug-in represents each category of effects. If you find several plugs listed for a single category, then the reason for this is among the following:

- My favorite plug-in is currently only available for one of the two VST computer platforms, so that I included the best possible alternative for the other platform.
- There are so many cool plug-ins available for a given category that I couldn't find it in my heart to settle for one and keep you in the dark about the rest.
- Next to the ›best‹ plug-in, there are one or more nifty alternatives that come fairly close but will cost you substantially less than my first choice.
- Because I wanted to.

A brief introduction to each section describing the type of effect will let you decide whether or not a plug-in of this nature is suitable for the way you think and work before you wade through the entire section.

▶ Under ›**Available in VST Racks**,‹ you'll find remarks describing to which of the VST effects racks a given plug-in can be loaded. Keep in mind that only if the plug-in comes in a stereo in/out version can you use it as a master effect.

As in real life, not everything that is possible is also sensible. Check out the comments in the line titled ›Standard Routing.‹ These remarks will tell you which type of standard signal routing option is best for patching the plug-in into the signal path. This is also valuable info which will let you decide if the plug is suitable for the manner in which you prefer to work.

Room Simulation

The effects type that is traditionally given the generic term
›reverb‹ is presumably the most important effect of them all.
The plug-ins discussed in the following section all simulate
space and thus add depth to a signal. Not only do the highlighted plugs give you plenty of detailed control options, they
all deliver excellent audio quality.

Good reverb plug-ins are among the most expensive software effects. Nevertheless, if you choose to buy a hardware
effects device with comparable capabilities, you'll find that
these cost three to four times what you'll fork over for a plug.
For most of us, the real thing—i.e. carting our gear around
to cathedrals or caverns—is not an option.

In terms of flexibility and sound, the plug-ins featured in
this section seriously out-perform the internal VST plug-ins
ESpacial and WunderVerb 3. However, the internal effects—
particularly WunderVerb 3—beat even the best commercial
plugs hands down in one aspect: they run on minimal CPU
power.

The bottom line is as simple as it is unfortunate: a reverb
that makes the grade for the most discerning high-end productions requires loads of computing power. If you are running VST on a computer that just barely meets the minimum
requirements for the program and load a high-end reverb to
your box, the performance of your system will suffer. Sooner
or later, it's bound to run out of steam.

Waves TrueVerb

VST Windows	DirectX	✓
	VST PC	—
VST Macintosh	✓	
Available in VST Racks	Send Effects, Channel Inserts and Master	
Standard Routing	Send Effects (Post-fader)	
World Wide Web	http://www.waves.com/	

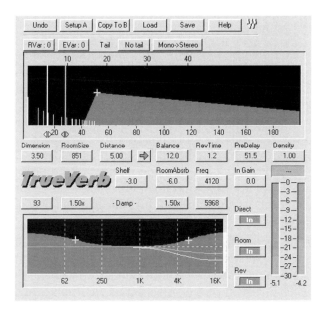

Concept

TrueVerb in particular is not your run-of-the-mill reverb, it delivers true room simulation. Its designers obviously went to great pains to make it emulate natural sounding rooms as realistically as possible, whereby you have plenty of options for tweaking parameters.

Two graphical elements mirror every parameter change that you make. What's more, you can move and shape most parameters directly via mouse.

Time Response

The time-related parameters are illustrated in the diagram above. At the bottom of the diagram, you can see a scale featuring milliseconds and at the top, a scale featuring meters. These give you the low-down on time-related parameters, for example lets you know that a reverb tail is 100 milliseconds long or the listener is hearing the signal 30 meters distant from the sound source.

◆ The sound source is symbolized by a line at the left border of the diagram. By moving the blue line, you can determine the room size (50 to 20,000 sq m). The other movable line represents the listener, who can be located from 0.5 to 40 m from the direct sound source. Not only can you use the yellow line to position the listener within the room that you have defined (left of the blue line ⇨ listener line is yellow), but also outside it (right of the blue line ⇨ listener line is red). What does this sound like? Similar to hearing the sound source ›funneled‹ through a window— somewhat more indistinct yet tighter.

◆ The actual effects signal is represented graphically through two elements: a number of white lines symbolize the individual early reflections and an area shaded purple depicts the level of the reverb tail. The following holds true for both displays: the higher the point on the graph, the louder the signal.

◆ You can select different basic patterns for early reflections (E Var), otherwise they are adjusted automatically according to the other parameters. You can vary oodles of parameters for the reverb tail, including the balance (level in relationship to that of the early reflections), starting point, start level, decay time and density. When Link mode is active (the blue arrow below the display points to the right), the reverb tail automatically responds to the room size and listener's position.

Frequency Response

◆ In the bottom diagram, you can determine the frequency response of the signal components. The thin blue (reverb tail) and yellow (early reflections) line form a frequency response curve that remains constant over time. In addition, the diagram depicts a large area shaded purple. It represents the frequency response curve as a function of time, whereby the reverb tail moves ever closer to it as it decays.

◆ In the output section, you again have the option of activating and deactivating the direct signal, early reflections and reverb tail separately as well as combine them freely. You'll find this an invaluable tool when you're fine-tuning the mix.

Rating

TrueVerb is the flagship of Waves' Native Power Pack. With its many parameters and highly detailed handled options, it allows you to work incredibly precisely when you are creating rooms and different types of reverb. The downside is that the many options may be a source of confusion to newbies.

The graphical user interface is great; it will immediately whet your appetite for building your own virtual rooms. Whereas normally you would just turn the reverb down if you find it too conspicuous, here you'll be inspired to experiment and try stuff like making the room smaller, moving the listener closer to the sound source or damping the reverb's frequency response curve. The cool thing is all that it takes to execute these types of operations is a simple mouse click.

The effects quality of TrueVerb is excellent—in my opinion it remains the crème de la crème of all VST plug-ins. However, you will only be able to really enjoy this plug-in if you own a fast computer. The amazing quality of TrueVerb's reverb effects demands a tribute—a serious amount of computing power.

To give you an idea of what a healthy appetite the plug-in has, consider this: to run properly, it requires the computer resources of four internal VST Espacial reverb plug-ins. To belabor the point, bear in mind that the extremely frugal VST reverb WunderVerb 3 requires just half of the computing power of the Espacial. In practice this means that on a high-end computer, you'll be able to run four or so TrueVerbs in realtime, in mid-class boxes, just one or two. If you own anything punier than a Pentium 200 or Ppc 604e/160, pass on the TrueVerb until you invest in box that packs a bit more punch.

Tips & Tricks

Chock full of features and parameters, the TrueVerb's many options are both a blessing and a curse. You'll find that it is easy to inadvertently dial in a setup that doesn't make a great deal of sense in terms of practical application. Particularly keep an eye on the three blue buttons at the bottom of the diagram just to the left of the level meter. These determine which signals TrueVerb outputs. What's the ›right‹ setting? It depends on the application:

♦ SEND: In most cases, you'll load TrueVerb to the SEND EFFECTS rack and route signals to it via the SEND circuits of the individual audio channels. If you chose this signal routing option, be sure to switch the DIRECT button in TrueVerb off. Otherwise, the ›dry‹ signal is routed through to the plug-in's output. You'll hear overlapping direct signals, which colors the tone of the signal, giving it a washed-out sound and weakening the reverb effect.

▶ Ignore this rule only when you are routing signals to the plug in PRE-FADER mode and the audio channel fader is pulled all the way down.

♦ INSERT: If you want to insert TrueVerb into the audio channels or the MASTER EFFECTS rack, usually you'll prefer to mix the dry or direct and wet or effects signal at the plug-in's output. In this case, you'll have to activate the DIRECT button.

You can determine which effects signals TrueVerb outputs via the other two buttons. For natural sounding reverb, always activate early reflections (EARLY REFL.) and reverb (REVERB) at the same time. A reverb signal without early reflections rarely makes musical sense. However, the opposite—

EARLY REFL. on, REVERB off—is handy trick for adding a touch of 3D depth without laying on distinctly audible reverb. Try slapping some early reflections on the drums of a dance track or laying them over vocals. While you're at it, experiment with the parameters EVAR, DIMENSION, ROOM SIZE and DISTANCE.

▶ If you make the TrueVerb generate early reflections only, you can come up with some pretty spacey flanger-like effects sounds. Give this a shot: Set DIMENSION to 1.0, DISTANCE to 2.0 and then drag the blue line (ROOM SIZE) from left to right for some freaky phasing fun!

▶ In VST Macintosh, you can even automate the parameter sweep. This won't work in VST Windows because the requisite Waves plug-ins are available in DirectX versions only and as we now know, DirectX doesn't do the automation thing.

Tc Works Native Reverb

VST Windows	DirectX	✓
	VST PC	✓
VST Macintosh	✓	
Available in VST Racks	Send Effects, Channel Inserts and Master	
Standard Routing	Send Effects (post-fader)	
World Wide Web	http://www.tcworks.de/	

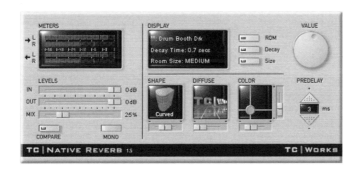

Concept

Like all other plug-ins by Tc Works, Native Reverb sports truly appealing 3-D visuals. It's features are arranged very clearly and the program is a piece of cake to handle.

Its interface is divided into three sections. At the left, you'll find a display for in- and output levels, the corresponding faders below it and a MIX fader that determines the balance of the wet and dry signal. By clicking on the COMPARE button, you can undo the previous operation.

At the bottom right of the diagram, you'll see three graphical displays. These let you determine the basic reverb parameters. The left box determines the room shape (circle, irregular oval or square). The middle box lets you influence the density of the reflections, a process which is labeled ›Diffuse‹ on the graphic.

In the box at the right, you can vary frequency response. Simply reposition the bull's eye in the box until you like the sound that you're hearing. Similar to a joystick, here you are simultaneously manipulating two parameters. To give you a visual indication of how the sound is being colored, the color of the bull's eye varies between red (›warm‹) and green (›cold‹).

There are just few other parameters that you can—or more accurately, must—manipulate numerically or via data wheel. These include:

◆ PREDELAY, which is automatically linked to the room size,

◆ DECAY, and

◆ SIZE, which is variable in nine increments.

Rating

Currently, the Native Reverb is presumably the TrueVerb's greatest competition—the main contender for the title ›Heavyweight Champion Reverb Plug of the World,‹ which is why a direct comparison is in order.

With a substantially greater number of parameters, the TrueVerb is certainly the more flexible of the two. It racks up points simply because it gives you more reverb characteristics to play with. On the other hand, the Native Reverb does a fine job of meeting all the requirements you might have for emulating natural rooms. Its quality may not be equivalent to that of TrueVerb in all respects, but it does come very close when you compare the majority of available features directly.

Most users will probably prefer to work with an interface that is clear, concise and easy to handle. The relative simplicity of Native Reverb's user interface earns the plug bonus points. In marked contrast to TrueVerb, newbies will immediately feel comfortable working with it.

Here's another point in favor of Native Reverb: From Version 1.5, this plug-in's performance was optimized so that it requires even less computing power. For example, you can run up to three Native Reverbs simultaneously in Vst Windows on a Pentium 200 Mmx. Sadly, the same setup can deal with just a single Waves TrueVerb.

The bottom line: TrueVerb is considerably more versatile, but Native Reverb is much easier to handle and conserves Cpu resources. Particularly for newbies—who generally don't start off with the most powerful box on the market—Native Reverb is highly recommended as an alternative to the more entrenched TrueVerb.

Tips & Tricks

With the parameters DIFFUSE and COLOR, you are controlling a fairly large value range within small graphics. Because it's so easy you'll be tempted to explore extreme settings. By all means, feel free to experiment, but if you're trying to come up with ›musical‹ results, keep the following in mind: usually the settings that venture ›close to the edge‹ but don't push at the far reaches of the parameters work best.

Note that the diverse versions of the Native Reverb plug-in differ slightly. For example, you'll find the MIX fader exclusively in the special plug-in version designed for the VST MASTER rack. On the other hand, you can only use the MONO button when you are processing stereo files in another DirectX-compatible host software.

◆ For example, when you're attempting to come up with a suitable DIFFUSE setting, it's a good idea to start with a fader position fairly close to the far left for rooms that you want to create for percussion instruments, whereas a position closer to the far right generally gets the job done for balladesque vocals, where longer reverb rooms work best.

◆ When you're tweaking COLOR, avoid the extreme bottom left position for drum loops because at this position the bottom end is over-emphasized in the reverb signal. If you slap this type of room on a kick drum, the results will generally be too muddy and lacking punch because there's too much ›drum‹ and not enough ›kick‹ in the reverb signal.

With its clear structure, the Native Reverb seems predestined for the following ultra-expedient short cut method of dialing cool reverb sounds—simply select a ROM preset and modify it manually. Although administering RAM presets in VST is a bit ›tricky,‹ starting with Version 1.5 the standard sixteen RAM programs per bank are possible:

1   A mouse click on the black bar at the bottom of the plug-in opens the menu listing the ROM presets. Activate the function USE OLD PRESET HANDLING located at the bottom of this list.

2   Under FILE, you can now save (SAVE EFFECT) the current plug-in setting for the VST effects device in which the Native Reverb is currently active and load it later (LOAD EFFECT).

3   Be sure to leave the plug-in parameter field open for these SAVE/LOAD operations.

Timeworks Reverb 4080L

VST Windows	DirectX	✓
	VST Pc	—
VST Macintosh	—	
Available in VST Racks	Send Effects, Channel Inserts and Master	
Standard Routing	Send Effects (Post-fader)	
World Wide Web	http://www.sonictimeworks.com/ index.htm	

Concept

The user interface of this plug-in for DirectX was inspired by the visuals of high-end analog reverb units. Its basic control features are:

◆ an internal BYPASS button,

◆ a knob that lets you determine input level, and

◆ a level display in the form of a VU meter. A switch located next to the meter lets you determine if it displays the input (IN) or output level (OUT).

◆ On the right side of the interface, you can see separate faders for the output level of the reverb (VERB) and direct signal (DRY). This option definitely comes in handy—it lets you use the plug as an insert or master effect.

The sound-shaping section consists of four faders in vertical array. They let you determine the PRE-DELAY of the reverb tail, DECAY, DAMPING and ROOM SIZE.

The COLOR knob enables you to influence the basic characteristics of a given room. What you are actually manipulating here is the ›hardness‹ of the sound—i. e. the treble content—and density. Most parameters are abstract values, so your best bet is to go by ear—tweak them so they sound best to you.

The 32/64-Bits button is a selector switch that lets you determine the internal resolution of the algorithm and thus the effects quality: 64 bits give you the best possible reverb quality, but also require substantially higher Cpu performance.

Rating

The control features of the 4080L are more than commendable. In a perfect world, all plugs would be as well-designed as the less than imaginatively named 4080L. Although the Tc Native Reverb's options for manipulating the reverb parameters are a tad cooler, here too, the clear, concise layout makes handling a piece of cake and lets you work intuitively.

In 32-bit mode, the 4080L requires just a trifle more Cpu power than the Tc Native Reverb, in 64-Bit mode, the power requirements range between those of the Tc Native Reverb and Waves TrueVerb.

In my estimation, the reverb quality is roughly comparable to that of the Tc Native Reverb. The performance of the 4080L is less impressive when it emulates the type of very small rooms often required for drums and percussion. For these applications, you need some type of control over the early reflections, which alas the 4080L does not give you. For medium to large rooms with damping typical of ›balladesque‹ reverb sounds, the Timeworks plug-in certainly delivers the goods.

Tips & Tricks

Although the Timeworks manual claims different, I believer there is a distinctly audible difference between 32- and 64-bit mode. Frankly, you should only invest in this plug if you can run it in 64-bit mode without having to worry about annoying performance bottlenecks—your setup should be powered by at least a P200 Mmx.

However, this mean average that only the 64-bit mode will give you decent results. You'll find that in 32-bit mode the reverb has a considerably grainer, brittle and thus harder sound. Particularly for drum and percussion rooms, these lower-fi sounds can be very useful and desirable. When in doubt what mode might deliver the best results in a given scenario, simply switch back and forth between operating modes and let your ears be your guide.

► The Timeworks product line features other DirectX plug-ins, including a highly recommended phaser. On the included Cd-Rom, you'll find demo versions of the Timeworks plug-ins. These are fully functional programs that you can try out for a period fourteen days. Definitely take advantage of this offer so you can judge for yourself.

Delay

Generally, when most users are shopping for this breed of effect, they aren't looking for much more than a simple echo device. Since the internal VST Stereo Echo plug-in already gets this job done, many an inventive plug-in designer took its concept a step further.

If you are looking for something a little spicier than something that basically repeats the original signal at variable intervals—say you want to use a delay plug-in to actually create grooves—give this little tool a try.

NeuroSonic GrooveDelay

VST Windows	DirectX	—
	VST PC	✓
VST Macintosh	✓	
Available in VST Racks	Send Effects and Channel Inserts	
Standard Routing	Send Effects (Post-fader)	
World Wide Web	http://www.neurosonic-systems.de/	

Concept

With the GrooveDelay package, you actually get two plug-ins:

◆ GrooveDelay is a leaner version of the deluxe module. Its advantage is that it chows down on less RAM and—because it passes on the frills and sticks to the essential parameters—is a great deal easier to handle.

◆ GrooveDelay Xᴛ is the ›e**XT**ended version,‹ a fully-loaded Gᴛ with bucket seats, blower, four on the floor and candy apple red paint job (so to speak).

On the user interface—possibly inspired by too many afternoons watching Star Trek repeats—you must first enter the desired song tempo in Bᴘᴍ. The bottom edge of the window features sixteen red Tᴀᴘ buttons, each of which represents $\frac{1}{16}$ of $\frac{4}{4}$ bar. A somewhat inconspicuous array arranges these in four groups of four, each group reasonably enough representing a quarter note.

By clicking on one of these buttons, you can activate a delay that matches the tempo of the song. The distance of a given button from the left edge of the window determines the delay rhythm.

Example: For a simple $\frac{1}{8}$-beat delay, skip the first two buttons and activate the third button from the left. For a delay in a $\frac{1}{4}$ time, skip the first four buttons and click on the fifth button from the left.

You can simultaneously activate as many buttons as desired to come up with more complex grooves where the delay patterns overlap. Below each button, you'll find a parameter each for the volume level and panorama position of the type of delay activated by a given button.

As usual, Fᴇᴇᴅʙᴀᴄᴋ lets you determine the length of the delay sequence, i.e. how often each Tᴀᴘ is repeated.

To make things even more complicated, the length of a Fᴇᴇᴅʙᴀᴄᴋ loop is not automatically an entire bar—you can also vary its rhythm via the S parameter. The G parameter lets you add a dash of ›human error.‹ However, we'll class the effect that this parameter generates as ›esoteric‹—other less forgiving folks might have said ›useless‹—and leave it at that.

The Xt version of the plug-in gives you more stuff to play with such as the parameters SAMPLE (T) and DYNASENSE. With the former, you can freely define the duration of a delay. For example, you could generate a delay with a $\frac{1}{4}$ groove, which is however muted after an $\frac{1}{8}$ interval—which is really a variation on a gate effect. DYNASENSE defines a threshold for level control of the effect, for example so that only the loud snare hits within a drum loop trigger the delay.

Rating

The user interfaces of both plug-ins not only look hip in a Warp 9 kind of way, they're also easy enough to figure out, which, in my book, deserves kudos every time. The diverse options for editing parameters let you work quickly and effectively—hats off to the masterminds behind the plug-in.

Less fortunately, the concept and parameters are not exactly crystal clear—it does take some effort and time to figure out what all of the stuff does. A peeve I have with the ›GrooveDelay Xt‹ is that the SAMPLE (T) parameter is not scaled in note values, which would have made handling much easier. The response of the DYNASENSE function could also be a bit more sensitive—in many cases, you'll probably think something along the lines of ›To hell with it,‹ and use the stripped-down plug-in version ›GrooveDelay‹ instead.

Despite its indisputable qualities and the fact that this is a totally unique program, GrooveDelay is not standard equipment in every Joe's and Jane's plug-in arsenal. If all you need is a simple tempo delay that delivers basic quarter or eighth note repeats, the internal Vst delay or the highly recommend freeware by Dave Brown (see page 223) or Digilogue (see page 232) will do just fine.

For everyone else who likes to put on the lab coat and spend hours creating complex grooves with the help of rhythmic delays, then GrooveDelay is an absolute must. I particularly recommend this plug-in to ambitious sound alchemists, musicians who have a jones for experimental electronics as well as dance and techno producers.

Tips & Tricks

To keep frustration down to a level where scenarios featuring handguns and bullet holes in your screen remain fantasy—albeit of the gratifying variety—you should work step by step and get a feel for each parameter in isolation:

1 Definitely earn your wings with the less complex ›GrooveDelay‹ first and be sure to route signals to it via SEND. Select input material that gives the delay plenty of ›room to breathe,‹ e.g a simple $\frac{1}{4}$ snare drum. To keep on top of what is going on, definitely activate the VST metronome click or play back some other type of simple, very unambiguous rhythm track along with the groove that you are tampering with.

2 Set FEEDBACK to zero. Initially, work with one TAP only. Not until you get the hang of it should you start experimenting with TAP combinations.

3 Go back to the single quarter note TAP and check out what FEEDBACK does in combination with different five values.

4 Set up a combination using all parameters of ›GrooveDelay.‹ Not until you can identify the influence of each parameter and know what happens when you tweak it should you move up to the more advanced ›GrooveDelay XT.‹

5 Here too, start out with a simple quarter-note delay without FEEDBACK to get to the bottom of the parameters SAMPLE (T) and DYNASENSE in isolation.

6 Again, set up a combination using all parameters, but be patient. ›GrooveDelay XT‹ features a bunch of options that won't become clear to you until you've worked with it for a good while.

▶ If you simply set all TAP VOLUME parameters to the peak value (99), the effect generated by GrooveDelay—depending on the input material—may sound too chaotic with just two active TAPS. Be sure to make liberal use of the VOLUME parameters of the individual TAPS to maintain some degree of sonic clarity.

▶ Define the effect or loop with one or two main delays by turning up their VOLUME values. Fill in the gaps with faster delays and turn their levels down to suitable, less dominant levels. If you use different PAN values to separate the individual TAPS in the stereo spread, you can come up with delays that sound fat and complex without a nervy or chaotic edge to them.

Parametric and Graphic EQs

Like the internal Vst EQs, the following filter plug-ins are all tools that let you manually manipulate tonal parameters. The difference is that these plugs offer more convenient handling options and, more importantly, substantially better sound quality.

Nevertheless, considering their miserly performance requirements, the EQs that ship with Vst are pretty good really—they do the trick for many users. Before you fork over the dough for one of the plug-ins highlighted in this section, you should ask yourself if you really need more flexible EQing options and better sound quality. If so, by all means go for one of these.

Bear in mind that all of these plug-ins by third-party vendors require substantially greater Cpu performance. As typical Insert effects, you won't be able to use these simultaneously for as many channels as the internal Vst EQs. Particularly for this reason, a preferred application for high-quality EQ plug-ins is processing stereo master files during mastering.

T

Steinberg/Spectral Design Q-Metric

Vst Windows	DirectX	✓
	Vst Pc	✓
Vst Macintosh	✓	
Available in Vst Racks	Send Effects, Channel Inserts and Master	
Standard Routing	Insert or Master	
World Wide Web	`http://www.spectral-design.com/`	

Concept

Q-Metric is a parametric filter with seven frequency bands. Its features and filtering characteristics are designed to deal with three classes of frequency bands:

◆ MID: The three mid-range bands are fully parametric, which means that you can control the cutoff frequency (16 Hz to 20 kHz), gain (max. ± 20 dB) and filter quality (Q-factor: 0.3 to 9.6).

◆ SHELF: The Q-Metric features one shelving filter each for the low and high frequency ranges. Instead of the Q-factor, you can select slopes of 6 and 12 dB.

◆ CUT: It also has one CUT filter each for the low and high frequency ranges on board. These let you surgically remove higher (HIGH CUT) or lower (LOW CUT) frequency ranges from signal. As far as playing with parameters goes, here you can only select the slope (6 or 12 dB) and control the cutoff frequency.

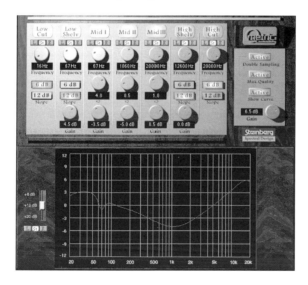

The buttons arrayed on the upper edge of the window let you activate each band separately. In the stereo version, you can also determine if the selected band influences the left channel only, right channel only or both simultaneously.

By clicking on the SHOW CURVE button, you can view the frequency response curve generated by the current parameter knob settings. Like a good EQ should, the scalable graphical display immediately mirrors every parameter change.

The features highlighted thus far are nifty, but nothing to write home about—you would expect much of the same from any decent EQ plug. What makes this plug-in special has to do with the buttons located on the right side of the parameter box. Here you can select whether or not the plug-in works with double the internal sampling frequency, an option judiciously called DOUBLE SAMPLING. In addition, the equally aptly named MAX QUALITY button lets you select the highest possible quality for the DOUBLE SAMPLING algorithm. This of course demands a great more from the CPU, but it does what it the name promises.

Rating

The graphical interface of this plug-in is arranged clearly and has an appealing look. In contrast to say Waves Q10, parameters cannot be edited directly via mouse in the frequency response curve, which may irritate some users.

However, bear in mind that the actual purpose of Q-Metrics is to emulate the tone of good analog filters as realistically as possible. The technical trickery used to do this is—at least when you get down to the nuts and bolts of tweaking frequencies—is of a secondary nature. Here are the factors that I consider relevant:

◆ The sound quality of this plug-in is truly excellent. The filter sounds wide open yet articulate and—at lower Q values—gratifyingly ›creamy.‹ To my ears, it measures up to considerably more expensive EQ plug-ins on other platforms (e.g. Focusrite d2 for TDM).

◆ Its signal processing wizardry demands a serious tribute in terms of CPU power. If all bands are active at the highest level of quality, the Q-Metric requires more computing power than any other VST plug-in I've come across. However, you will generally only need some of the available frequency bands, which in turn conserves computer resources. If even then the plug-in drains your computer dry, than of course you can always switch it to ›normal quality.‹ However, in this mode the plug-in doesn't deliver nearly as persuasive a performance—you might as well use other EQ plug-ins.

If you are looking for a filter plug-in primarily for sparse acoustic recordings and/or mastering applications, this plug will definitely have you singing its praises. In terms of tone, Q-Metric is the luminary amongst VST compatible plug-ins. Again though, you wouldn't want to invest in Q-Metric unless your computer has enough horses under its hood to this plug justice.

Tips & Tricks

For every active band in Q-Metric, you have to pay a price in terms of computing power even if you set its GAIN control to 0 and thus doesn't do any signal processing per say. Always make sure that the ACTIVE buttons at the top of the window illuminate only for those bands that you actually need.

If you want to filter the two sides of a stereo file differently, you have to use some of the bands for left and other bands for the right channel. In contrast to some other EQ plug-ins, Q-Metric does not enable you to dial in different parameter settings for the left and right channels in a single band.

If you want to use all bands to process each stereo side, you should first filter one channel, use track bouncing to write your EQing data to the audio file and then filter the other channel as a separate step. Although this process is not what you might call convenient, you'll rarely have to use it in practice since it isn't all that often you EQ the two sides of a stereo signal differently.

Q-Metric is one of the few plugs that is available in all three VST compatible formats in an all-included package. You can thus run the VST Pc plug-in formats that can be automated in VST Windows and the DirectX version in an audio editor.

Tc Works Native EQ

VST Windows	DirectX	✓
	VST Pc	✓ (EQ-P)
VST Macintosh	—	
Available in VST Racks	Send Effects, Channel Inserts and Master	
Standard Routing	Insert or Master	
World Wide Web	http://www.tcworks.de/	

EQ-G

Concept

This package actually features two EQ plug-ins, a graphical (EQ-G pictured in the illustration above) and a parametric filter (EQ-P pictured in the illustration below). Both plugs come in a DirectX version and the EQ-P also in the VST Pc format.

This makes a great deal of sense simply because the option of automating parameters—which the DirectX plug-ins lack—is particularly important when you're working with the parametric EQ. Here it is available for a maximum of four frequency bands.

Much of the stuff on the user interface will already be familiar to as it is comparable to the Tc Works Native Reverb. In the following, we'll take a look at some of the more unique features of these two plug-ins:

Parametric EQ

Here you get seven fully parametric frequency bands with individually variable filter characteristics (PARAMETRIC, HIGH/LOW SHELVING, NOTCH). You can determine the quality (Q: 0.1 to 4.0) or slope (3 to 12 dB/octave), cutoff frequency (20 Hz to circa 22 kHz) and GAIN (max. 18 dB) for each band. If desired, you can control the GAIN and BYPASS circuit separately for the left and right stereo channels. LINK lets you do just that to the two stereo sides, link them.

EQ-P

At the upper right corner of the window, you'll find a ›joystick‹ designed for global EQing. It allows you to influence two parameters simultaneously:

◆ TREBLE (vertical): Boosts or cuts high frequencies (flat shelving filter from 4 kHz) by a maximum of 6 dB.

◆ LOUDNESS (horizontal): Does the same for the bottom end at 250 Hz and high end at 6 kHz at the same time. This feature lets you effortlessly determine the amount of ›presence‹ that you want a sound to have.

As a visual aid, the plug comes with a display that indicates the resultant frequency response in different colors for the right/left channels. All parameter changes—regardless if you make them via the diverse bands or joystick—are mirrored immediately in the display.

Graphic EQ

You can select 7, 14 or 28 frequency bands for this filter. All of the bands can be edited directly via mouse in a large display, either individually or globally in linked mode. At the left of the window, you'll find a large fader. Its purpose is to allow you to vertically compress or expand frequency response as indicated in the display.

In contrast to its parametric cousin, EQ-G always influences both stereo sides by an equal measure—meaning of course that you can't EQ the left or right signal side individually.

Another interesting feature found on both EQ plug-ins is called SOFT SAT. This handy little tool prevents digital distortion when you boost frequencies beyond the saturation threshold. If you inexplicably like digital grit, you can switch this automatic damping function off.

Rating

This EQ package is unquestionably the most versatile amongst the VST compatible plug-ins—you get two different breeds of filter plug-ins, each designed for different sound-sculpting purposes. With the Native EQs, you have what it takes to get the EQing job done:

- For one, the ›iron fist‹ that you at times need to pulverize unwanted frequencies and bend sounds radically—a task at which the Waves Q10 excels;

- for the other, a tool that lets you unobtrusively ›sweeten up‹ the sound—in other words, the kind of hi-fi embellishment of the entire mix that mastering usually calls for.

This is what the Steinberg/Spectral Design Q-Metric does best it.

In both applications, the Native EQs are not quite up snuff with the sound of highly specialized plugs, but they come close enough for my money. What's more, this package meets all sound-sculpting prerequisites—a primary consider-ation if you're on a tight budget—whereas the higher-end plug-ins can only cover some of them.

In terms of CPU power, the Native-EQs are neither perfor-mance guzzlers nor misers, kind of in the middle, I'd say. The more sophisticated EQ-G—especially when you're using it for numerous frequency bands—requires roughly twice the CPU resources of the EQ-P. Like with all TC-Works plug-ins, handling is exemplary—everything is clearly arranged and sussing stuff out is a piece of cake. Plus you get some unique features that sets these plugs apart from the competition. All in all, I can whole-heartedly recommend the Native EQs as a universal EQ package.

Tips & Tricks

On TC Works plug-ins for the computer platform Windows, you'll often find extremely helpful functions concealed be-hind the right mouse button. When you're working with the EQ plug-ins, you'll find it much more expedient to click on the following elements via the right mouse button:

◆ TOUCH SCREEN (EQ-G): Lets you freely draw EQ curves. The individual bands are automatically adjusted to mirror the stuff you're drawing.

◆ BAND PARAMETER (EQ-P): Here you can copy a select para-meter or all parameters of a band to any one of the other six bands or all bands simultaneously.

◆ COMPARE (both EQs): This function calls up a pop-up menu in which the last twenty operations are documented. By selecting a given entry, you can restore the status of the

EQ at a given stage of your editing process. Now if some-one could only make this work in real life.

- ◆ BUTTONS/SLIDERS: Lets you view a Help text explaining a given function.
- ◆ LEVEL METERS: Selects and controls the Peak Hold func-tion (the highest most recent values remain visible).

By the way, these last two items do the same thing in other Tc Works Windows plug-ins such as the Native Reverb.

Waves Q10

VST Windows	DirectX	✓
	VST PC	—
VST Macintosh	✓	
Available in VST Racks	Send Effects, Channel Inserts and Master	
Standard Routing	Insert or Master	
World Wide Web	`http://www.waves.com/`	

Concept

Waves Q10 is a fully parametric EQ, or more accurately, an entire bundle of EQs. Along with the ›fully loaded‹ Q10 plug-in featuring—you guessed it—ten frequency bands, the pack-age comprises the ›leaner‹ versions Q1, Q2, Q3, Q4, Q6, and Q8. It probably doesn't come as a complete surprise to you that each of these plugs features the amount of bands indi-cated by the number following the ›Q‹. Other than the num-ber of bands, everything else in these versions is identical.

You can switch each filter band off and on individually, which is a great help when you're ›auditioning‹ complex fil-ter curves. Every filter band features three parameters:

- ◆ TYPE: Reasonably enough, this selects the filter type via icons—BANDPASS/NOTCH, LOW- and HIGHPASS as well as Low- and HIGH-SHELVING are available;

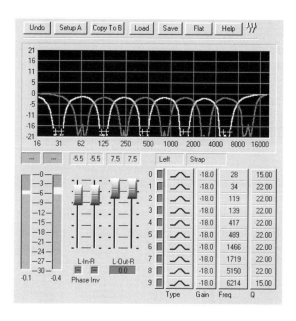

◆ GAIN: amount of amplification/attenuation (maximum ±18 dB);

◆ FREQUENCY: cutoff frequency (16 Hz to circa 22 kHz);

◆ Q: Q-factor or Slope (0.5 to 100).

All numeric parameters—in the classic Waves plug-in style—can be controlled via mouse or entered directly using the computer keyboard. In the stereo versions, all band-specific parameters for both channels can be linked (STRAP) or controlled separately, including the filter type!

The top portion of the window always displays a graphical representation of the filter curve that is generated by the current settings. In it, you can point to the diverse filter bands directly and move these as you see fit. In Stereo mode, the frequency response curves for the left and right channels appear in different colors.

Rating

Q10 is a solid EQ package, sans frills. Although even the puniest version of the Q plug-ins requires more computing muscle than the internal VST HIGH QUALITY EQs, you get what you pay for—these EQs are definitely more precise and well-articulated.

Nevertheless, the tone of the Q10 is not going to be everyone's cup of meat. Particularly when you're mastering, you'll find that there are plug-in voicing sections that sound silkier and more subtle. On the other hand, this filter does a great job when you really want to warp the hell out of a fist full of frequencies. The highly variable as well as extremely wide range of Q-factor settings, coupled with the option of overlapping filter bands at will let you really wreak havoc on the frequency response. You could even say its capabilities make it a sound design tool. Particularly its aptitude for bending synth sounds makes it a must-have for every techno freak's production arsenal.

As far as handling goes, the Q series has its ups and downs: On the one hand, most digital audio enthusiasts will enjoy the large and thus user-friendly frequency response display and the option of manhandling EQ bands directly in the graphical display. On the other, the interface has a distinctly unhip technical and now somewhat antiquated look.

By the way, the look and feel of the DirectX and VST Macintosh versions vary slightly. Whereas on a Windows PC you can see every change displayed immediately in the frequency curve when you move individual bands, on a Macintosh the curve doesn't follow your movement until you release the band. Although this difference seems minor, its effect is considerable: the DirectX versions are much easier to handle.

On the other hand, the DirectX versions cannot—in contrast to the VST Macintosh plug-ins—be automated. If your system runs on the Windows platform, you might want to consider that in this aspect, the plug-in falls short of the com-

peting products Tc Native Eq and Steinberg/Spectral Design
Q-Metric.

Tips & Tricks

Evidently, Waves' rationale for the many different Q plug-ins
is that the smaller versions require less computing brawn.
Sounds fair enough, but other manufacturers manage to do
the same with just a single plug-in version—in these, only an
active frequency band actually consumes Cpu power.

If this might lead you to surmise that the Q plug-ins are not
particularly intelligent in terms of conserving resources, you
would be absolutely right. If you go for this plug-in package,
be sure to keep the following in mind:

◆ An active Q10 plug-in always draws the same amount of
Cpu power, regardless if you have activated none, one or
all ten frequency bands.

◆ Certainly, a Q2 plug-in requires considerably less Cpu resources than a Q10 plug-in. Logically enough, this may
lead you to assume that the Q10 requires five times the
resources of the Q2. However, in practice this supposition
does not hold water. The difference in resource requirements is not nearly as dramatic.

If you ambitiously start Eqing with the Q10 and find that
you can get the job done with fewer frequency bands, you
can activate one of the leaner Q plug-ins and spare computing resources:

Save the settings as a PRESET via the internal Q10 function
SAVE TO NEW FILE. Activate the Q plug-in that features the
number of bands that you actually need and load the PRE-
SET.

▶ Note: Although you can use the plug's internal File functions to swap
PRESETS among the Q plug-ins, the program is unable to localize the
active bands automatically. For example, say you activated Bands 1
and 8 in Q10 and saved this setup as a PRESET. When you load this PRE-
SET in a Q2 plug-in, it will only be able to identify Band 1.

If you save exactly the same setup in Q10 but use Bands 1 and 2 instead, you can load the PRESET as is. For this reason, you should make a habit of activating the requisite frequency bands in sequence. In other words, never skip a band. You won't have any trouble sticking to this scheme as every Q10 band can be assigned freely to any desired frequency range!

When you're working with these plug-ins, you'll find that—as so often is the case with virtual gizmos—some of the functions are somewhat inconspicuous. A case in point is the option that lets you edit the frequency response graphic directly:

◆ You can see which of the frequency bands is represented in the graphic by simply clicking on it. The corresponding number in front of the band parameters at the bottom will appear in red.

◆ Only when you move an *active* frequency band in the graphic will you get audible and visible results. In the DirectX versions, it suffices to simply move it from the zero position to activate a band directly in the graphic. In VST Macintosh, you can switch it off and on in the graphic by pressing and holding the ⌘ key down while clicking on it with the mouse.

◆ You can vary the Q-factor by moving a band while holding the ⟨alt⟩ key down. You thus have direct graphical access to all relevant band parameters.

Use this technique for the Q-factor to make a complex filtering effect that processes several overlapping bands sound softer or more aggressive!

◆ You can ›round up‹ several bands simultaneously: Use the mouse to draw a ›corral‹ around the ones you want to select or click on them while holding the ⬆ key down. Then all changes that you make will affect the selected bands proportionally.

▶ The Q10 comes complete with a comprehensive preset library. When you have a spare moment, be sure to check out the diverse ›pseudo stereo‹ settings. In these, the input signal is shaped by filter bands that process the left and right stereo channels via different symmetrically staggered frequency bands. Mono input signals end up sounding wider, more spacious and all it takes is a bit of frequency bending to achieve this effect.

Steinberg/Spectral Design Free Filter

T

VST Windows	DirectX	✓
	VST PC	—
VST Macintosh	✓	
Available in VST Racks	Send Effects, Channel Inserts and Master	
Standard Routing	Insert or Master	
World Wide Web	http://www.spectral-design.com/	

Concept

Free Filter is certainly the most unusual plug-in discussed in this section. Its capabilities can roughly be classed in three categories:

◆ GRAPHIC EQ: In its first ›incarnation,‹ the plug-in is a ›normal‹ graphic EQ featuring thirty frequency bands. These can be switched from LINear to LOGarithmic via selector buttons. Thirty faders enable you to shape the filter curve, which is displayed graphically in the top portion of the window. At the bottom left of the screen, you'll find a TOOLBOX equipped with three graphical mouse tools. Although these don't enable you to draw directly in the frequency response graphic, they do give you relatively flexible options for shaping the curve, which in many cases is much faster than manhandling the many faders individually.

◆ ANALYZER: The display window not only depicts the current filter curve (yellow), but also the frequency spectrum of both the input signal (green) and the output signal (red) as influenced by the current filter curve. Rather than being displayed as an average value, the input and output signals are shown dynamically—in other words, the display responds in realtime.

◆ FREEZE: This button enables you do just that—freeze the display at any time. This is actually a pretty nifty little tool—it lets you take a closer gander at any song position that you might for whatever reason think is worth further study.

◆ LEARN: Lastly, the most spectacular feature of the bunch: With these buttons located at the top edge of window, you can have Free Filter analyze two frequency spectra, compare them and compute the resultant filter curve. You can thus use any audio file—say a track on your all-time favorite CD as the SOURCE, analyze it and then use your own mix as the DESTINATION. After the program has analyzed the source track, you can bend the frequencies of the destination track to emulate the source as close as you care to. In other words, this is a license to steal mixes.

Rating

Available for a number of years now, the TDM plug-in ›IQ‹ by Intelligent Devices works along similar lines. The concept behind Free Filter is not new, but it is nevertheless ingenious and totally unique among VST-compatible plug-ins.

Despite its many features and functions, Free Filter is not a universal tool that will help you master every EQing task under the sun. To belabor the obvious, a 30-band EQ such as this one works with many extremely narrow frequency bands. Ergo it tends to color the sound somewhat more than a typical mastering EQ with just a few bands. For the job that some audio engineers call ›sweetening‹—a barely perceptible boost of high-end frequencies during mastering—something along the lines of the Q-Metric is the considerably more suitable tool. This explains why Steinberg/Spectral Design decided to offer two filter plug-ins—we're talking apples and oranges here.

Nevertheless, Free Filter is an extremely versatile EQing tool. With its integrated analyzer capability, the plug is a viable alternative to the Waves analyzer plug-in PAZ (see page 196).

As sceptical as you might have been when you read about the LEARN function, you won't be disappointed if your expectations aren't wildly unrealistic. If however you have your hopes set on analyzing a CD produced by ›insert favorite studio guru here‹ and hearing your mix sound exactly the same after just a single mouse click, be prepared for some serious disillusionment. You're probably well aware of the fact that the qualities of a good mixdown are not determined solely by the average frequency spectrum. Many other factors such as the arrangement, phase response, pulse response (transients) and 3D imagery, just to name of few of the more important ones, play decisive. What Free Filter can do is make your mix sound a bit more like the track you are trying to model it on, which is pretty groovy too.

In my opinion, the greatest advantage of this feature is that it helps you understand how the Joe Pro mixes tracks. Particularly if you're a newbie, using Free Filter regularly will help you learn the tricks of the trade. It enables you to see and hear what your mixdowns are lacking or which frequency ranges are over-emphasized when you compare them with the work of people you respect.

▶ All other qualities aside, Free Filter definitely deserves honors as the ›No. 1 Learning Tool‹ among Vsт compatible plugs.

Tips & Tricks

Possibly inspired by my rave review, you are probably raring to find out for yourself how Free Filter will help you become a mix master virtually overnight. No problem, just follow these simple steps and you'll be on your way to fame and fortune—maybe:

1 Record a track from your favorite Cd to Vsт, or better yet, import it directly from the Cd using a suitable utility program.

2 In Vsт, load the audio file to a stereo track and position it next to your own mixdown.

3 Use Free Filter as an insert effect in the stereo channel or as a master effect.

4 In Free Filter, activate the Source button and play back the reference track. Take your time—Free Filter will be able to come up with a more representative analysis if you give it a minute rather than say five seconds.

5 End the analysis via a mouse click on the Learn button and stop the track.

6 Follow much the same procedure to analyze your mixdown: Click on the Dest button and play back your file. The length of the analysis should roughly be equivalent to the amount time you gave Free Filter to analyze the reference file.

7 End the analysis via a mouse click on the Learn button and stop the playback.

8 Click on the Match button. Free Filter computed a filter curve that represents the difference between the two files and now displays it for your viewing pleasure.

9 Play your mixdown file back. Use the MORPH fader to determine how far you want to bend your mix to emulate the computed filter curve. You can actually view these changes as the shape of the filter curve changes accordingly.

10 Here less is definitely more: If you don't go overboard, the results will generally sound more authentic, less artificially colored—in a nutshell, better.

11 When you drag the mouse cursor over the frequency response curve, the current position is indicated numerically in Hz and dB. Try to scope out which frequencies have the greatest influence on the sound of the mix. Try to identify which frequency ranges were over- and under-emphasized in your mix.

12 If necessary, you can also use the ›standard‹ tools (band fader and toolbox, see above) to edit the computed filter curve manually.

The L/ST/R buttons at the bottom of the window also have a significant influence on signal processing. For example, if you activate L, the right stereo channel is muted in the plug-in. Although this comes in handy for monitoring purposes, when you are processing stereo files, make sure that the ST button is always active.

Now that the ›main features‹ have hogged the plenty of limelight, let's take a quick look at the LIN/LOG buttons. Although relegated to a low-man-on-the-totem-pole position at the bottom of the window and dwarfed by the rest of the features, there are some critical functions hiding behind the unassuming front. Bear in mind that when you activate one of these, you are not only changing the characteristics of the spectrum display, but also the distribution of filter bands and thus the entire sound of the Free Filter.

In LINEAR mode, all frequency bands have exactly the same width (for example, at an audio sampling rate of 44.1 kHz, 700 Hz per band). In LOGARITHMIC mode, the filter bands have ›musically meaningful‹ intervals, thirds to be precise. Here a lower frequency band is thus much wider than a higher frequency band. Particularly when you're creating filter curves manually, this mode is generally your best bet.

Psychoacoustic Filters and Enhancers

The difference between the ›normal‹ EQs discussed in the previous section and the class of signal processors introduced in this one boils down to:

◆ A ›normal filter‹ can only manipulate frequencies that are actually part and parcel of the input signal.

◆ A so-called ›psychoacoustic filter‹ analyzes the input signal and computes ›suitable‹ overtones, subharmonics and similar stuff. Here existing frequencies are not only cut or boosted, totally new frequencies are added to the signal.

The reason the algorithms used for this purpose are called ›psychoacoustic‹ is not because of their consciousness-altering qualities—the programmers simply took into account how the human brain perceives sound. This type of effect is usually deployed when normal EQs are unable to deliver the desired results.

The following plug-ins will help you make the most of certain kinds of audio material. Although some of the more ›esoteric‹ competing products make the same claim, you'll find the quality of the results is often dubious. Nevertheless, keep in mind that the effect of these plugs is rather subtle, and well it should be. If you go to task with too heavy a hand, the results will range from mildly annoying to truly ugly.

Steinberg/Spectral Design Spectralizer

Vst Windows	DirectX	✓
	Vst Pc	—
Vst Macintosh		✓
Available in Vst Racks	Send Effects, Channel Inserts and Master	
Standard Routing	Insert or Master	
World Wide Web	http://www.spectral-design.com/	

Concept

This plug-in generates second and third harmonics based on the input signals. In other words, it adds overtones for a more expansive, shimmering sound. As you can see in the illustration above, the plug features relatively few control features, which makes it pretty easy to get a handle on. The focal point of the window consists of five faders:

◆ INPUT: Master control for the input level of the plug-in, which means that when you are using the plug as an insert effect, this fader also influences dry signals that are routed through the plug.

◆ GAIN: Think of this feature as an input level control for the plug's frequency analysis section. It can be used to boost the input level to an even higher level. The greater the gain, the more intense the effect.

◆ 2ND/3RD: These two faders influence the level of the added second and third harmonics, respectively.

◆ MIX: Determines the effects balance. When this fader is pulled all the way down, you will hear the dry signal only. If you push it to the peak setting, the maximum amount of harmonics that the plug is able to generate is added to the signal.

Although they are somewhat ›overshadowed‹ by the large fader section, the smaller control features located in the top portion of the window are responsible for crucial functions:

◆ FREQUENCY: It lets you determine the cutoff frequency (1 to 7 kHz)—the portion of the audio signal that lies above this threshold is analyzed. The lower the threshold, the more pronounced the effect.

◆ DENSITY: In increments from 0 to 6, you can vary the ›amplitude envelope‹ of the generated harmonics. Here too, higher values increase the intensity of the effect, but only when you are patching in percussive input signals. When you're working with signals that have a relatively level amplitude (pads), the effect is hardly discernible.

◆ KICK: This feature gives you yet another option for increasing the intensity of the effect when you're processing percussive input signal. When you activate it, more overtones are generated during the attack phase (e.g. the initial snap of a kick drum) than for the remainder of the signal, so that you end up with an even punchier sound.

◆ SOLO: When you activate this switch, you will hear only the generated harmonics sans the dry signal. This is an invaluable aid when you are trying to determine the right settings for the remaining parameters.

On the right hand side of the window, you'll find a level display, which—if I had my way—would be mandatory for all plugs, and a CLIP LED, which gives you a visual indication of internally overdriven signals. Try to make a habit of keeping an eye on both of these.

Rating

The Spectralizer is easy to handle and delivers exactly what its makers claim it does. With this plug-in, you can inject that elusive, expensive-sounding ›shimmer‹ into your mix—just the secret ingredient that makes the difference between a fair and a goose bump-inducing sound.

With added overtones, the processed audio material often sounds more expansive, transparent and crisper. The plug is great for restoring audio material marred by a lack of overtones. If something sounds stale and muddy, go ahead and give it shot with some of your older recordings, lo-fi samples or even vintage vinyl LPs.

In contrast to simply boosting the high frequencies via a filter, you can use this plug-in to actually re-synthesize frequencies that the signal is lacking, either because it never had them to begin with or were lost in previous processing or recording operations. Not only does its special algorithm set the Spectralizer apart from simple ›enhancers,‹ the option of adding punch to percussive material via the KICK feature also wins big bonus points. Here, and coincidentally in all other processing operations that the plug is capable of, you'll be delighted by the fact that the algorithm does not add any audible noise.

As usual, superior performance demands a tribute in terms computing power. The Spectralizer's appetite for CPU resources is not quite as voracious as the that of the Waves TrueVerb, but it comes close enough for discomfort. However, this is not all that great a gripe because you will generally employ the plug-in for post-processing finished stereo mixdowns.

Another persuasive argument in favor of the Spectralizer is its relatively affordable price. When the plug-in debuted, it ran on the ProTools/TDM platform and cost a whopping 2,000 DM. In comparison, the VST version is a bargain.

Tips & Tricks

If you want to make the most of the Spectralizer, it is essential that you understand how the sound-shaping parameters interact. Particularly the following two observations are well worth bearing in mind:

◆ The FREQUENCY setting has a decisive influence on the overall sound: For example, if you set a value of 3,000 Hz, the plug will only generate additional overtones for input signals' frequency ranges down to 3 kHz. Ergo, the second harmonics added by Spectralizer always lie above 6 kHz (2nd harmonic = double the frequency = 1 octave higher),

◆ the thirds above 9 kHz (3rd harmonic = triple the frequency = $1\frac{1}{5}$ octaves higher).

If one of your drum loops lost some of its zest after you processed via lo-fi, retro or modulation filter plug-ins, you can put some sizzle back into it via the Spectralizer: Switch the KICK function on, set DENSITY to 5 or 6, FREQUENCY between 1 and 4 kHz depending on the audio material, and presto, the punch is back!

◆ When you're going for a ›natural‹ sound, you should always set the 2ND fader to a higher setting than the 3RD fader. If the effect sounds too aggressive at this setting, set a higher FREQUENCY value. For a mix that already sounds pretty good, generally values no higher than 6 or 7 kHz deliver the best results—a subtle, very silky top end. If the effect is no longer audible at these settings, you can turn up the GAIN fader to boost the analysis stage and raise the level of the effect.

Here's a rule of thumb that should serve you well: Whenever you are varying parameters, be sure to occasionally switch the plug to SOLO mode. This is the only way you can distinguish between high-end frequencies that are inherently part of the dry signal and frequencies that you are synthesizing via the plug. Think of this feature as the style police—it will keep you from making overzealous mixing decisions. Remember, just enough tweaking is a sign of good taste, too much and your mix will wear the aural equivalent of green polyester golf slacks with matching tassel loafers.

Waves MaxxBass

VST Windows	DirectX	✓
	VST Pc	—
VST Macintosh	✓	
Available in VST Racks	Send Effects, Channel Inserts and Master	
Standard Routing	Insert or Master	
World Wide Web	http://www.waves.com/	

Concept

MaxxBass was—in case its picturesque name left you in any doubt—designed specifically to make the most of the bottom end. It is based on psychoacoustic phenomenon that has to do with something called ›missing fundamentals‹ by some:

What MaxxBass does is analyze the portion of the input signal that lies below a variable frequency threshold and based on this information, generates overtones. These overtones fool the human ear into believing it is ›hearing‹ extremely low fundamentals that aren't actually there. Not only does this bit of trickery put one over on your ear, it also dupes speakers into to reproducing frequencies that sound like they are well below what the specs indicate that they can handle—in the case of the MaxxBass, up to two octaves below the rated handling capacity.

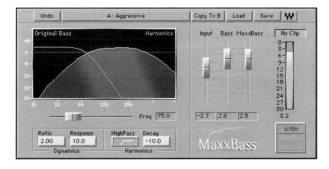

In the right section of the window, you'll find three faders that give you direct access to the key components of signals:

◆ INPUT: Yep, the input signal

◆ BASS/ORIG BASS: The portion of the dry signal that lies below the defined threshold. This is the frequency range that the plug analyzes. The results are used to compute the effect signal.

◆ MAXXBASS/HARMONICS: The effects signal generated by the plug-in.

The button at the bottom right corner of the window mutes the direct signal so you can monitor the two effects signals on their own.

▶ In MaxxBass jargon, the standard operating mode is called AUDIO: Here the signal consists of a mix of the input signal and effects signal generated by the MaxxBass, the balance of which you can determine at will.

The graphical display on the left side of the window is a co-ordinate system indicating level (vertical axis) and frequency (horizontal axis). In the display, you will find two curves:

◆ ORIGINAL BASS (left/blue): This is the part of the original signal that is analyzed. You can redefine the threshold of the input signal via the FREQ fader—the MaxxBass ignores the portion of the input signal that lies above this threshold. The BASS fader influences the level of the curve.

◆ HARMONICS (right/yellow): This curve represents the computed HARMONICS. The level of the curve is determined by the MAXXBASS fader.

HIGH PASS and DECAY let you further narrow down the frequency range of the effects signal. Finally, the DYNAMICS parameter controls the on-board ›upward compressor.‹ It lets you tweak the tone of the virtual bass so that it sounds ›lazy,‹ ›laid back,‹ ›punchy‹ or anything in between.

Rating

Unfortunately, MaxxBass is not an audio wizard that enables you to scoff at the laws of physics and turn a Hofner Violin bass sound into bone-crushing techno thunder. You are not going to squeeze mighty subbass signals out of a tinny multimedia speaker. What it will help you do is—particularly for compact, sonically limited sound reproduction systems—come up with more articulate bass sounds and aurally more appreciable fundamentals.

The type of effects that this plug-in is capable of producing are unique—I'd venture it is almost obligatory for anyone who mixes or masters audio for Internet publishing, computer games or other multimedia applications.

I recommend this plug highly for processing audio material designated for reproduction in fixed installations—in other words, sound reinforcement systems where the characteristics and limitations are known quantities. Here too the plug will allow you to some extent transcend their physical limits, for example by helping you to come up with even more impressive and clearly audible subsonic effects for theaters.

If you want to use MaxxBass solely for mastering normal audio CDs, I'd say you'll be able to survive without it. Here the plug-in can in many cases be a hip alternative to a conventional EQ, but you'll have to use it sparingly. You want the results to sound good on as wide a variety of audio systems as possible, so you'll have to settle for the compromise that you feel most comfortable with.

Having said that, if the subbass range plays a crucial role in your productions, I would recommend the MaxxBass. There will in most cases be an audible albeit relatively subtle improvement in the sound of your tracks.

Tips & Tricks

The two HARMONICS parameters located at the bottom right of the control panel are key factors in shaping the character of the effect produced by the MaxxBass. You'll find a filter icon at the left. The flatter this filter, the lower the generated ›virtual‹ fundamentals will be. You have three slopes to chose from:

◆ 12 dB/octave (flat): ideal for multimedia,

◆ 24 dB/octave (medium): standard setting, e.g. for CD audio,

◆ 24 dB/octave (steep): good for eliminating D.C. in signals and special effects such as subsonic Fx for theaters.

The second parameter (DECAY) determines the threshold for the HARMONICS. If you choose too high a setting for this threshold (around –9), you may end up with a track that sounds mushy over smaller speakers. A lower threshold (towards –24) delivers better results when you hear the track piped through high-quality speakers simply because the sound is more crisper and articulate. On the other hand, with a low threshold, the effect may be too feeble to be appreciable over multimedia speakers. So here too, some type of compromise that you can live with is in order.

When you're working with material destined for multimedia applications, you should always consider the circumstances under which these systems operate: Inexpensive multimedia speakers without a subwoofer are normally rated for a lowest frequency between 110 and 150 Hz. When you maximize audio material via the MaxxBass for this type of speaker, it's a good idea to try to ease the load of the woofer as much as possible because it is already operating at its limits. This means that you should:

1   Mute the original bass signal completely.

2   Set a frequency threshold to a value in the range of 110 to 150Hz via the FREQ fader. Use a set of typical multimedia speakers as your monitors and identify at which point you can still hear a difference between the dry and wet signals.

3 Try to narrow down the range of generated overtones (HARMONICS) as much as possible. For this purpose, set the high pass filter to the steepest position and the DECAY parameter to the lowest value so that you come up with as ›hilly‹ a HARMONICS curve (yellow) as possible.

This setup will deliver the best results for extremely limited speakers.

▶ A freeware alternative to the MaxxBass is available from Maxim. The SubBass Synth plug-in generates a similar audio effect and is also available in Macintosh and Pc versions.

Modulation and Synthesis Filters

These effects may seem very similar to the EQing tools we had a look at earlier, but in this case appearances are indeed deceiving. For one, the following plugs are all ›resonance-capable.‹ They are thus closer related to the filter circuits that are used to shape sounds in synthesizers and samplers.

Another huge difference is that these plugs all feature on-board modulation options. What this means is that you don't have to settle for a static effects sound. These let you sculpt sounds dynamically without having to use VST parameter automation. Sounds—depending on the input material—can be modulated by another audio signal or even an LFO synced up to the song tempo. These are primarily used for bending the blaze out of sounds, sound design in general and exploring the outer limits of the sonic universe.

Waldorf D-Pole

VST Windows	DirectX	—
	VST Pc	✓
VST Macintosh		✓
Available in VST Racks	Send Effects, Channel Inserts and Master	
Standard Routing	Insert or Master	
World Wide Web	http://www.steinberg.net/ products/plugins.html	

Concept

Although the D-Pole is officially called a ›Filter Module,‹ the description is far too humble. With its diverse effects sections, this plug could easily pass as a combination tool. Its concept, visuals and sound were obviously modeled on Waldorf's hardware filter ›4-Pole,‹ whereby you could say that the D-Pole—equipped with several nifty features that the 4-Pole lacks—outclasses the original.

The control features are arrayed in six sections, all labeled by terms highlighted in orange bars:

◆ FILTER: Its basic function is obviously filtering, whereby you can vary the CUTOFF frequency and RESONANCE. You can choose from five filter types, each of which can operate with a slope of 12 or 24 dB.

◆ AMP: Here you can not only determine the volume and panorama of the effects signal, but you can also distort it (OVERDRIVE) and add delay (DELAY MIX).

◆ OSC: When you turn up the RINGMOD knob, the you will create ring modulation between the input signal and an oscillator signal generated by the plug-in. The other parameters of this effects section let you vary the waveform, frequency and routing of the ring modulation effect.

Depending on the oscillator waveform, this section will produce anything from syn-drum to fuzz-like effects. You can also vary the pitch of the effects signal via FREQUENCY.

◆ DELAY: This is a simple delay; you can vary the delay TIME, FEEDBACK and high-frequency DAMPING. When you activate CROSSED, the effect works like a ping-pong delay. To determine the level of the delay signal, go to the AMP section (see paragraph above).

◆ ENV: The Cutoff MOD knob lets you define the intensity of the input signal level's influence (›Envelope Follower‹) on the filter frequency (CUTOFF). Sounds complicated? It's not really: Use this effect to create gate-like effects or have the filter kick in only in response to loud snare hits within a drum loop. DECAY determines the rate at which the filter closes.

◆ LFO: This little component livens up the proceedings considerably. It generates an oscillator signal for which you can determine the frequency (SPEED) and waveform to modulate several of the parameters we just had a look at. The potential modulation destinations are CUTOFF (basically a filter frequency sweep), PAN (the effects signal roams through the stereo image) and OSC (the pitch of the ring modulator effect changes). You can control the intensity of the modulation individually for each of these three effects.

In addition, you'll find two more knobs at the left of the panel which are not assigned to any of the sections discussed earlier. Nevertheless, each has a crucial function:

◆ SAMPLE RATE: With this knob, you can turn down the sample rate of the input signal as low as you like. This is a classic ›lo-fi effect,‹ which depending on the setting, delivers anything from a brittle to metallic sound.

◆ TEMPO: Set this knob to the tempo of the current VST song, then when you're tweaking some of the other parameters, note values such 1 BAR or $\frac{1}{8}$ will appear along with the frequency values. This is a pretty practical feature—it lets you set the delay times and LFO speeds to ›musically meaningful‹ values.

Rating

The quality of the different sections varies. The delay sounds, which are generally easy enough for digital effects to generate, are good. The filter—undoubtedly the most important component—sounds excellent, as does the ring modulator.

Although sound of the distortion section and sample rate conversion suffers in comparison—the modifiers static and inanimate come to mind—including these sections nevertheless made good sense. Why? Simply because the strength of the D-Pole lies in its ability to combine different effects, modulate them and make something greater than the sum of its individual parts when these interact.

Of course its many components make the D-Pole fairly challenging for inexperienced users. Nevertheless, even newbies should soon get the hang of it because its programmers evidently put some thought into making it relatively easy to handle.

I can't complain about its performance either. Its appetite for Cpu power is about average for commercial plugs, which is admirably modest considering the variety of effects combinations that it is able to deliver.

Once you understand what all of the ingredients do and how they ›taste‹ when you toss different combinations of these into your sonic stew, you can use the D-Pole to cook up an incredibly wide-ranging menu of modulation effects. It will deliver anything from subtle emphasis on the dynamics of a signal to syn-drum effects, from grooving and pulsating pads to brutal Björkesque lo-fi effects. I happen to be someone who loves this kind of stuff, so I'll have to admit I have a soft spot for the D-Pole. Actually, forget objectivity, it's one of my all-time favorite Vst plugs.

Tips & Tricks

The manner in which the different effects sections interact is extremely complex. You should start with a neutral basic setting, which conveniently is the default when you call the D-Pole up. First explore the Filter sections and after you feel comfortable working with these features, reset the parameters to neutral values (Cutoff max., Resonance min.). Follow

Unfortunately, this plug-in does not allow you to enter numeric parameter values directly. If you decide to go for the D-Pole, before you start twiddling knobs, be sure to read the tips on editing parameters graphically on page 32!

the same procedure and experiment with AMP, DELAY, OSC and SAMPLE RATE separately(!). Not until you have a handle on all of this stuff should you brave the modulation options of ENV and LFO.

Once you have become truly confident working with the plug, you can try some more advanced trickery: Some of the parameter value ranges on the D-Pole are more then generously apportioned, which if you decide to exploit this potential, lets you come up with truly unusual effects. For example, try the following with a drum loop:

◆ DELAY: Set DAMPING to 0, FEEDBACK to an extremely high or low value, and vary TIME in the lower range, say between 0.09 and circa 25 ms. This will produce some ugly but nifty comb filtering effects.

The LEDS ACTIVE and BYPASS are located in the AMP section. Bear in mind though that BYPASS does not just affect the status of this section, but actually the entire D-Pole. The only knobs that remain active are AMP VOLUME and AMP PANNING. Actually, BYPASS works the same way it does on all other devices, but on the D-Pole it's a little harder to locate!

◆ LFO: Here the SPEED values range substantially higher than what you might be accustomed when using an LFO to modulate signals. Try setting the LFO SPEED to somewhere in the range of 4,000 to 7,000 Hz, the waveform to TRIANGLE, CUTOFF MOD to around 50, and in the Filter section, the 12-dB Lowpass CUTOFF to circa 400 Hz and RESONANCE to something in the neighborhood of 70. This setup alone will produce some pretty vigorous lo-fi distortion. Now try combining this configuration with a lower SAMPLE RATE and OVERDRIVE, and knock yourself out twiddling the CUTOFF MOD knob. If you crank the volume on your system, I'll wager it won't take long for your neighbors to pack up and head south for the winter!

◆ RING MOD: Turn ring modulation well up, OSC FREQUENCY to circa 700 Hz, ROUTING PRE, SLOPE SAW. Now set the LFO SPEED to a musically appropriate $\frac{1}{16}$ time and goof around with the OSC-MOD knob: voilà—automatic scratching. If you grow bored with playing spin doctor, bend the effect via an ENVELOPE modulation (turn the FILTER CUTOFF down and ENV CUTOFF MOD up—or vice versa).

Opcode fusion:Filter

VST Windows	DirectX	✓
	VST Pc	(in the works)
VST Macintosh		(in the works)
Available in VST Racks		Send Effects, Channel Inserts and Master
Standard Routing		Insert or Master
World Wide Web		http://www.opcode.com/products/ fusioneffects/

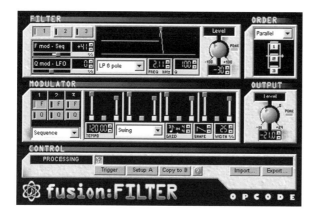

Concept

This plug-in features freely definable combinations of three independent filter sections with loads of modulation possibilities. You can determine how you want to combine the filters—in other words, the order of the filters in the signal chain. Five possible options are accessible in the ORDER box.

Three buttons in the FILTER section are used to select which of the filter units you want to work with. The remainder of the user interface automatically displays the requisite control features.

As far as filter characteristics go, you have a heap to choose from—fifteen to be precise. In addition to low- and high-pass filters with varying slopes, you also get four different ring modulators and a distortion unit.

You can enter the standard parameters such as gain, frequency and Q-factor numerically. Even more conveniently, you can manipulate the filter directly via mouse in the graphic adjacent the parameters.

The cutoff frequency and another parameter (e.g. gain or Q, depending on the filter type) can be influenced by the MODULATOR section. The two MOD faders located on the left side of the FILTER section determine the intensity of the modulation. You also have a number of choices when it comes to the type of modulation:

◆ LFO: Here you can not only select the waveform (square, sawtooth, triangle or the ›random‹ waveform sample & hold) for the modulation oscillator, but also manipulate a number of other parameters.

◆ ENVELOPE: Unsurprisingly, here an envelope with a variable DURATION (max. of 100 sec) does the modulating. You can use the mouse to DRAW the desired curve or have it automatically follow the dynamics of the input signal (ENVELOPE FOLLOWER).

◆ AUDIO: With this feature, you can import any audio file from hard disk and have the modulation curve computed and patterned after this model. This lets you do stuff like patch in a synth pad as the plug-in's input signal and make it groove to the rhythm of a drum loop that you can import for use as a modulation source.

◆ SEQUENCE: Here you can first define a quantization raster by entering the basic tempo (BPM), time signature and note value. Then you can use the mouse to draw modulation pulses with different intensities. If this seems like an awful lot of work to you, you can instead load one of ten predetermined configurations for the SEQUENCE modulation.

The LEVEL knob in the FILTER section enables you to control the output level of each filter section individually and thus mix polyphonic modulation sounds.

Rating

Calling this plug-in a mere ›filter‹ is a classic understatement. The possibilities are many and so complex that I can only scratch the surface in this limited space. Not meaning to insult anybody's intelligence, but this plug-in is not recommended to newbies. You should have at least basic skills in dealing with complex signal and modulation routing, otherwise this plug will leave you hopelessly confused and extremely frustrated.

You could say that this plug was designed for much the same purpose as the Waldorf D-Pole—more the hey-let's-put-this-signal-through-the-audio-meat-grinder-and-see-what-comes-out-the-other-end school of effect. Nevertheless, the two plugs are markedly different:

The fundamental sound of the D-Pole filter circuit is clearly better. On the other hand, with its three relatively autonomous filter modules, fusion:Filter lets you conjure up sounds that are even more complex and polyphonic. Moreover, features like ›rhythmitizing‹ input signals via an imported audio file or drawing step sequences for modulations make fusion:Filter entirely unprecedented.

Newbies take heed—your best bet is to go for the D-Pole, it sounds a bit better and is much easier to handle. If you're a more advanced user, you will however have a ball with this plug—provided of course that you enjoy seriously mangling sounds. My advice to experienced hands in the digital audio game: Go for both, fusion:Filter and D-Pole.

▶ The performance of fusion:Filter gives no cause for complaint. However, its craving for CPU power gets voracious when you activate several entities of the plug-in. In practice, this won't matter much though—one fusion:Filter is complex enough to encourage premature aging, running several filters in parallel is akin to begging for a nervous breakdown.

More good news: Opcode has announced that in addition to the currently available DirectX versions, native VST formats are in the works. Presumably, this will take care of the multi-entity power gluttony problem.

Tips & Tricks

To ease your way into getting a handle on fusion:Filter, think ›baby steps.‹ Set up the three blocks in parallel and activate them one at a time as you become more familiar with the plug. Here's a good method to get you started:

1   Select the entry PARALLEL under ORDER.

2   You can change the status of the section by repeatedly clicking on the graphic: An active module appears yellow, a block in BYPASS mode blue and a grey block indicates that the signal is muted.

3   Activate Block 1 (yellow) only and mute the other two blocks (grey).

4   Experiment with Block 1 for as long as it takes to grasp the basics.

5   Once you feel comfortable working with Block 1, mute it (grey) and turn your attention to Block 2 (yellow).

6   Once you've ›dialed in‹ a cool configuration for Block 2, switch both 1 and 2 on (both yellow) to hear them in combination.

7   Proceed in the same manner with Block 3.

By clicking on a BPM parameter while holding the [alt] key down, its current value is automatically loaded to all BPM parameters of the other modulation sources. This is an indispensably practical short cut when you have created complex filter setups that give good groove and want to expeditiously adapt these to another song tempo.

Not to nag, but you should gain plenty of experience with this type of parallel filter configuration before you start dabbling with serial setups or mixing the two types of signal routing options.

Another item we should take a look at is the feature that lets you create LFO modulations based on tempo:

1   Select LFO mode in the MODULATOR section.

2   Select METER for SET RATE BY.

3   Enter the tempo of the current song in BPM under TEMPO.

4   Now you can enter the LFO frequency in musical note values. This option makes it incredibly easy to come up with precise rhythmic LFO modulations.

Vocoder

This section is a fitting follow-up to the preceding one—here too, we're dealing with filtration and bastardization of signals. A vocoder is in principle nothing more than a combination of an analyzer stage and a parallel circuit consisting of several band-pass filters.

The analyzer stage dissects the signal that you want to use as the modulation source (›modulator‹). It scrutinizes the different frequency bands and generates corresponding control voltages: If the original signal features lots of sizzle, the control voltages for the *upper* frequency bands increase. If on the other hand it booms, the vocoder cranks the *lower* control voltages.

The signal that you want to modulate—the ›carrier‹ signal—is piped through a combination of suitable band-pass filters. The level of these filters is determined by the control voltages generated in response to the frequency analysis. In this manner, the modulation destination is shaped by the tonal characteristics of the modulation source, which depending on the quality of the vocoder, sounds anything from shoddy to groovy.

You may have heard typical vocoder sounds such as ›talking synths,‹ but this breed of sound-sculpting toy can be used to achieve many other effects, for example to make a strings pad pulsate to the beat of a percussion track.

Opcode fusion:Vocode

Vst Windows	DirectX	✓
	Vst Pc	(in the works)
Vst Macintosh		(in the works)
Available in Vst Racks		Send Effects, Channel Inserts and Master
Standard Routing		Insert or Master
World Wide Web		http://www.opcode.com/products/fusioneffects/

Concept

fusion:Vocode features a classic vocoder algorithm, which in this case features five frequency bands. The plug-in input signal is the MODULATOR. In the CARRIER section, you can select which signal you want the MODULATOR to shape in its own image. You have two basic options for choosing CARRIER signals:

◆ PRESET: Here a simple on-board synth serves as the CARRIER. You can select an oscillator waveform from 23 presets (the classic waveforms, white noise, voices, strings etc.). On the graphical mini-keyboard (which lets you scroll through a whopping ten octaves), you can click on any desired chord.

◆ CUSTOM: Here you can import an audio file that you previously saved on hard disk and use it as the CARRIER signal.

If you like what you're hearing and want more of it, the EMPHASIS knob lets you do just that to the effect, emphasize it. DEPTH controls the overall intensity of modulation—in other words, the balance between the CARRIER and effects signal.

In the TONE section, you can fiddle with the five filter bands. Their frequencies are predefined, but you can manipulate the average level for each band. This lets you influence which frequencies are emphasized and thus shape the sound of the effects signal.

Rating

In comparison to a good analog vocoder, the five filter bands of fusion:Vocode are somewhat meager. Considering that it isn't exactly well-appointed, the plug-in delivers acceptable articulation—human speech is relatively intelligible, but Vocode certainly can't measure up to an analog vocoder.

One of the reasons for this is that the signal that it produces is at times tainted by artifacts, for example slight chatter or flutter generated by the effect. The few frequency bands that you have available also make it exceedingly difficult to come up with ›silky‹ yet articulate sound.

To enhance the vocoder effect, you will generally be forced to crank the upper frequency bands and the EMPHASIS parameter, which tends to give you a harsh or brittle sound.

Another major problem with the DirectX version is its miserable performance. The boys and girls at Opcode evidently agree, because they equipped the plug-in with a special ›Lo Fi‹ button that curbs its appetite for CPU power. However, the reduced sampling rate does a serious number on audio quality—they weren't kidding with the ›Lo Fi‹ label. Plus the plug still chows down on resources even when you're cooking on ›low flame‹—many computers won't be able to satisfy its cravings. For example, if you run Vocode under VST Windows on a Pentium 200 MMX, even in ›lo Fi‹ mode you won't be able to use it as a realtime plug-in, which kind of puts a damper on the fun you should be having.

All in all, I recommend Vocode conditionally: You should only consider buying the plug-in for VST Windows if you own a truly powerful computer and have run a demo version of the program on it to make sure Vocode runs smoothly before you buy.

Although a VST Macintosh version of fusion:Vocode is in the works, Macintosh users don't have to count the days waiting for it to be released. The fortunate Mac-o-philes can already enjoy a substantially hipper vocoder plug-in that runs on this computer platform—Orange Vocoder by Prosoniq.

Tips & Tricks

Indeed, the file import function lets you load any audio signal to Vocode and use it as the modulator as well as the carrier. However, only certain combinations of signals make sense when you're trying to achieve a vocoder effect:

◆ Using strings sounds as modulators is generally counter-productive. You should prefer dynamic signals—you know, the kind that sound like a party rather than a wake—drum loops, percussion tracks, speech, vocals etc.

◆ The carrier (File Import) signal on the other hand should ›hold still‹ long enough so that you can ›inoculate‹ it with the modulator signal—you want a relatively consistent sound so that you can hear the vocoder effect. Experiment with synth pads, ambient sounds, choirs or strings.

◆ The audio material doesn't have to be totally static. The effect is usually more interesting when the carrier signal is a bit more animated. However, any changes in the carrier should be extremely lazy—think ›slacker on valium.‹ For example, a synth sweep sound should open up ›veeer-rry slooowwly.‹

◆ Different filter bands are at work here, so the vocoder effect is most distinct when they are all employed gainfully. Particularly for the modulator, I recommend you use ›broad-band‹ sounds featuring a host of different frequency ranges. Come to think of it, the same holds true for the carrier.

▶ Vocode is equipped with PEAK LEDS; these are located next to the LEVEL knobs. In theory these should light up in bright red to alert you to internal clipping. However, they don't work flawlessly, so at times distortion is audible while the PEAK LEDS merrily continue to indicate all is well by remaining green. You're better off trusting your ears—if something sounds overdriven it probably is. Simply turn the LEVEL knobs down.

Prosoniq Orange Vocoder

VST Windows	DirectX	—
	VST PC	(in the works)
VST Macintosh		✓
Available in VST Racks		Send Effects, Channel Inserts and Master
Standard Routing		Send Effects (Pre-fader), Insert or Master
World Wide Web		http://www.prosoniq.com/

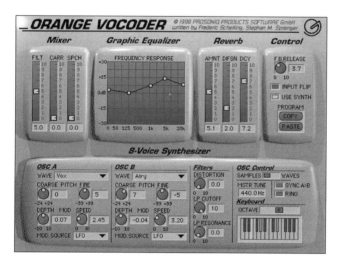

Concept

The Prosoniq Orange Vocoder works with an impressive 24 frequency bands and thus delivers very detailed resolution. Its interface clearly indicates that it means business:

♦ At the left of the control panel, you'll see a MIXER. It enables you to determine the balance of the different signal components FILTER (Vocoder effects signal), CARRIER (the dry signal that you want to modulate) and SPEECH (the dry signal that does the modulating, i. e. the ›modulator‹).

◆ You'll find a GRAPHIC EQUALIZER featuring a maximum of twelve frequency bands at the center of the panel. It lets you conveniently edit filter parameters directly in the graphical display.

◆ The plug gives you a REVERB section located at the end of the signal chain. You can set the basic reverb parameters AMOUNT (effects level), DIFFUSION (density) and DECAY (fade-out time) via faders.

Things start to get heady when you take a closer look at the CONTROL section. This is where you choose the carrier and modulator and tell them what to do: No surprises here regarding the modulator, it is the plug-in's input signal. The choices of carrier signal are similar to the options that Vocode gives you, with one major difference—these are a great deal more inventive:

◆ AUDIO: Here you can use another audio signal as the carrier. However, you don't have to import it from hard disk, you can if you choose use a signal on another VST track.

Sonic sorcery? Well, almost: the Orange Vocoder installs a special plug-in called VOC CARRIER for this purpose. You can plug this utility program into any other VST mixer channel as an insert. It ›taps‹ into the audio signal on the desired track and routes it internally to the ›actual‹ plug-in, the Orange Vocoder, thus enabling a VST track to provide the carrier signal in realtime.

◆ The INPUT FLIP button lets you swap the carrier and modulator around.

◆ SYNTH: As an alternative carrier, you can also draw on the signal produced by an on-board virtual synth, which you can access and activate via the succinctly named USE SYNTH button. It works with two oscillators that are able to generate variable waveforms (WAVES) or more complex samples (SAMPLES).

Moreover, you can play with parameters such as coarse and fine tuning for each oscillator—you even get an internal modulation option with variable speed, modulation depth and source. You can choose an Lfo, amplitude envelope or pitch envelope as sources, whereby the latter two are modulator-controlled. The oscillators operate in parallel, but you can also synchronize them or configure them as a ring modulator circuit.

◆ The virtual synth also comes complete with a modest low-pass filter section featuring controls for the Cutoff frequency, resonance and even an integrated distortion unit.

◆ Here too, you can define a chord on the mini-keyboard (max. of eight voices), which is then ›played‹ on the virtual synth.

Rating

It may seem a bit unfair to compare the Prosoniq Orange Vocoder and the Opcode fusion:Vocode—at the time of printing, the Orange was made exclusively for Apple platform (Vst Macintosh); the fusion:Vocode runs solely on a Windows-Pc (DirectX).

On the other hand, although Opcode has announced a Vst Macintosh version and ProSoniq a Vst Pc version are forthcoming, since these are the only two vocoder plug-ins *currently* available for Vst, a shoot-out was inevitable.

So there you have it, I had to let the two disparate plugs duel it out. The cold, hard truth is the Opcode was severely trounced—the Orange Vocoder won by a huge margin on points. The Prosoniq plug-in out-classed its opponent in every aspect:

◆ With 24 frequency bands, its sound is clearer, softer and more detailed.

◆ The interface is more clearly arranged, handling is easier.

◆ With a 12-band voicing section and a reverb section, it offers more sophisticated features, although you shouldn't expect sonic miracles from the reverb section.

◆ Alone the option of using a realtime signal as the carrier would have decided the match in favor of the Prosoniq plug-in.

◆ The internal synth of the Orange Vocoder actually deserves its name. It does a lot more than a simple mini sample player and sounds great.

◆ The performance of the Orange Vocoder is brilliant. In most cases, you won't exploit all of the available eight voices of the internal carrier synth at once. And if you don't, you can easily run the plug-in on medium to smaller Macintoshs.

The verdict speaks for itself. If you're in the market for a vocoder plug-in and own a Macintosh, go for it. VST Windows users will either have to wait for it to be ported or settle for fusion:Vocode. If the latter was what you had planned, sorry if I rained on your parade.

Tips & Tricks

If you want to patch in a carrier signal via the VOC-CARRIER plug-in, you will encounter a minor problem. When you use this program as an Insert effect in the mixer channel strip where you want to tap into the carrier signal, you will hear the dry carrier signal via this channel as well. In most cases, this is undesirable because you want to be able to mix the dry carrier signal on the Orange Vocoder mixer.

If this is how you are planning to route the signal, I recommend you load the VOC CARRIER plug-in to the Send effects rack. Send the signal from the carrier mixer track in PRE-fader mode and pull the channel fader all the way down. With this signal routing setup, you can mix all involved signal levels as desired and if necessary, even mix several carrier signals of different tracks together.

Compressors

A compressor is used to squeeze the dynamics of signals. It reduces the level of louder passages so the entire signal sounds more compact, punchier and on a subjective level, louder. With the exception of classical music, these attributes are all much coveted in all styles of music. Particularly productions designated for the dance floor or radio, where a punchy sound is obligatory, benefit from this type of processing.

Eqs and reverb ship with Vst, for a compressor you'll have to look elsewhere. Consequently, if you regularly record acoustic signals such as vocals, guitar, bass or drums, a compressor plug-in should be the first item on your shopping list. Even if you don't have much use for these ›natural‹ signals, a compressor will still come in handy. So before you invest in your umpteenth reverb plug-in, consider this—you'll get a bigger bang for your buck if you hand over your allowance for one the compressors introduced in the following section.

▶ If you are unwilling to invest in another plug-in, you can still have your virtual cake and eat it to. Happily, some kind souls programmed freeware compressor plug-ins designed to run under Vst. A few of these effects come in a quality good enough that will let you at least process individual tracks, for example vocals, where you can hardly do without compression. I recommend the Compressor plug-in by Dave Brown or KwickKomp2 by Syncromesh.

Waves C1

VST Windows	DirectX	✓
	Vst Pc	—
VST Macintosh		✓
Available in VST Racks	Send Effects, Channel Inserts and Master	
Standard Routing	Insert or Master	
World Wide Web	http://www.waves.com/	

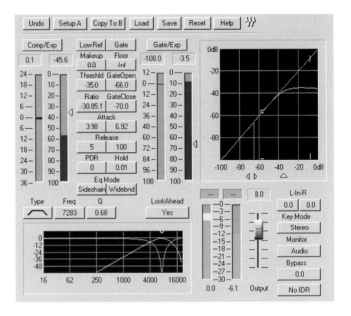

Concept

C1 is a kitchen-sink style effect featuring compressor, expander and gate functions, which the guys and gals at Waves confusingly crafted into five different plug-in versions. An in-depth explanation of the C1's deluge of parameters would easily provide enough material for another complete WIZOO Guide. At best, I can provide a cursory introduction to some of its vast potential:

The focal point of the user interface is a diagram depicting the current dynamics curve. It assigns a certain output level to every possible input level. Although you can't shape the curve directly via mouse, it does mirror every parameter change immediately.

Its signal shaping options comprise every crucial type of compressor parameter, including:

◆ ATTACK and RELEASE as well as PDR (**P**rogram **D**ependent **R**elease). This is an automatic, signal-dependent release control function used to influence the release rate,

◆ MAKEUP—makes changes in parallel to global level corrections,

◆ THRESHOLD—determines the point at which the curve dips off,

◆ RATIO—controls the degree of compression—in this case giving you extremely versatile control options.

With positive values (1:1 to 50:1), you can generate traditional compression, often called ›downward compression.‹

Values exceeding 50:1 are indicated as negative values −50:1 to −5:1. Here signal peaks that exceed the threshold are not only reduced to the level that the threshold is set to, but below it. This means that quieter passages become more prominent, while louder passages are more or less muted (CANCELLATION MODE).

At values lower than 1 (0.5:1 to 1:1), signal peaks above the threshold are boosted to even higher levels. This means that the dynamic range is not compressed, quite the contrary it is expanded (HIGH LEVEL EXPANDER).

The plug gives plenty of visual support when you're trying to come up with the right settings. At the left of the control panel, you'll see a COMPRESSION meter with variable characteristics. It moves in different directions and uses different colors to indicate the intensity of whatever type of signal processing operation—compression or expansion—you are currently working with. Next to it, you'll see a display for the input level—the little triangular slider lets you determine THRESHOLD.

To the right, you'll find exactly the same features for the GATE/EXPANDER section. A typical Waves output section with level meter and output fader is located at the bottom right of the panel.

One of the cooler aspects of the C1 interface is that the input level (located on the bottom horizontal axis) and output level (on the actual dynamics curve) appear as little white boxes that jump around autonomously depending on the status of the signal. This gives you a visual indication of where the level is currently at on the curve that you configured, when it exceeds the THRESHOLD and so forth.

The C1 GATE section is identical in terms of concept and handling—even some of the parameters are the same. Here's a quick look at the most important differences between it and the compressor:

- The THRESHOLD is not what you might be accustomed to— a single level at which the gate opens or closes. Here you can determine the GATE OPEN and GATE CLOSE levels separately. This lets you come up with something similar to a ›buffer zone‹ between the two levels to prevent the gate from ›chattering,‹ an undesirable effect caused by the gate rapidly muting and unmuting the signal.

- Next to GATE mode, you also get an EXPANDER mode. It allows you to attenuate the level below (CANCELLATION MODE) or boost it above (LOW LEVEL COMPRESSION) the GATE OPEN threshold. A separate parameter called FLOOR lets you vary this setting.

- Here, the time parameters ATTACK and RELEASE are supplemented with the parameter HOLD. It does just that to the gate—holds it open for a variable amount of time (10 ms to 5 sec). This feature is also used primarily to combat unwanted side effects such as chatter.

At the bottom edge of the full C1 version, you'll see an EQ section. Hardly coincidentally, its options are identical to that of a frequency band in the Waves Q10 EQ. The EQ in the C1 is however more than just an additional voicing section for the output signal, it actually expands the so-called SIDECHAIN functions.

Rating

Waves C1 was the first compressor plug-in on the market and is now considered a classic. In the age of the 30-second sound bite, this happens pretty quick. Anyway, this package gives you a comprehensive set of ingenious dynamics-related tools.

With its sophisticated functions, the C1 not only knocks out standard tasks such as compressing vocals or guitars with ease, but can also cope with truly difficult challenges such as refurbishing flawed recordings. It really can help you solve a wide range of audio problems, including eliminating undesirable background noise or separating specific parts of signals.

The user interface and displays—for that matter, its entire concept—are complex but consistent; they form an cohesive whole. The audio quality of the algorithms is very good. On the downside, the load it places on the CPU is also extremely high, particularly the DirectX version is a real resource hog.

If you have a solid technical background, aren't put off by an interface that looks more like it belongs on a high-tech measuring instrument in a nuclear power plant and occasionally enjoy implementing wacko ideas, then by all means, go for it. The C1 should be your first choice.

If this doesn't come close to describing your abilities and needs, and you only need a compressor for squashing the odd vocal track, I advise against this plug-in: the relative length of the section describing its concept hints at the intricacies of the C1.

The entire user interface has a very technical look and feel—if you're more the self-taught intuitive musician than a formally educated technician, you may have difficulty seeing the forest for all trees. Only if you know all about the different types of dynamics processing options and what they're used for, and the difference between them and what they do to signal levels, should you give the C1 a go. If this type of stuff is still a bit out your league, you may be inviting headaches you don't really need.

The bottom line: Technology junkies, go for it; newbies, hands off!

Tips & Tricks

Especially with the DirectX version, I can never remember which name goes with which C1 plug-in. A look at the Online Help (V. 2.5) suggests that its makers are equally puzzled by their own nomenclature. As much for my benefit as yours, here's a detailed list:

◆ C1+: the full version with all available functions, i.e. Compressor/Expander, Gate/Expander, SIDECHAIN and IDR (see page 192).

◆ C1: identical, except without IDR.

◆ C1/Comp: less of the same—here the Expander/Gate section went AWOL.

◆ C1 Compressor: the Compressor section, without SIDECHAIN and IDR.

◆ C1 Gate: Expander/Gate section only, without SIDECHAIN and IDR.

To offer some form of explanation of the SIDECHAIN function mentioned, we'll have to back up a couple of steps and look at the big picture. Normally, the input signal wears two hats at the same time in dynamics processing:

◆ CONTROL SIGNAL: The input signal influences the plug-in's dynamics functions. For example, when the input signal's level exceeds the THRESHOLD, this tells the compressor algorithm to go to work.

◆ PROCESSED SIGNAL: The input signal is influenced by the plug-in. For instance when a gate closes, the input signal is muted at the effects output.

These two roles can of course be assigned to two different signals: one controls the dynamics-related functions, the other is manipulated by these. This type of ›division of labor‹ is called SIDECHAIN mode.

In C1, you have access to this type of option via the so-called KEYING MODES. Whereas in early incarnations of the C1 it was reserved exclusively for ›pro‹ (= expensive) versions designed for ProTools/TDM and Sound Designer II, from Version 2.5, this Waves plug-in feature also ships with the native packages for VST Macintosh and DirectX. Enough rambling, if you do go for the C1, learning by doing will give you better idea of the SIDECHAIN mode anyway:

1 Run the C1+ version as a MASTER EFFECTS plug-in.

2 Go to the VST Audio Mixer and load a pad. PAN it hard left and select as spare a percussion loop as you can find and PAN it hard right.

3 In C1, start out with a neutral position (RESET). Here the KEY MODE (bottom right) is set to STEREO. This means that schizophrenia rules—the entire input signal serves both as the control signal and processed signal, which happens to be the standard mode.

4 Set KEY MODE to R → L. Now the left channel controls the right. Ergo the percussion loop is the control signal and the pad is being processed by it.

5 Now move the small blue triangle located next to the fourth upper level meters from the left. This changes the threshold of the GATE. When the level reaches this threshold, you will the hear the pad being muted to the beat of the percussion loop.

6 Sound like sonic garbage? Well, you passed the taste test! Seriously though, the point of this little exercise was solely to explain how the Sidechain function works and maybe inspire you to come up with something that sounds a bit better.

If this isn't complicated enough for you, don't worry, it gets worse. Now the EQ section comes into play, which was evidently conceived solely to enhance the SIDECHAIN function. With the EQ MODE buttons, you can determine how the EQ processes the signal.

- WIDEBAND: Although technically correct, its name doesn't tell you much about what it does, but I will—nothing. OFF would have been the more apt moniker because in this mode the EQ section plainly has no influence.

- SIDECHAIN: The sidechain signal is patched through the EQ before it drives the dynamic stage. If you allow only high frequencies to pass, the compressor will only respond to the high frequencies in the control signal. In KEY MODE STEREO, this feature turns the plug into a classic de-esser.

- SPLIT: Here the EQ not only splits the control signal, but also the processed signal into two frequency ranges. One part of the signal is allowed to pass, the rest is subjected to dynamic processing. You could also call this mode a ›dynamic EQ‹ because it processes the signal more or less heavily depending on the level of the filtered frequency ranges.

In the latter two modes, you can monitor the EQ signals separately, which is crucial when you are attempting to come up with just the right EQ settings. Predictably, this function is called MONITOR, you'll find at the bottom right of the C1 control panel.

Waves Renaissance Compressor

VST Windows	DirectX	✓
	VST PC	—
VST Macintosh	✓	
Available in VST Racks	Send Effects, Channel Inserts and Master	
Standard Routing	Insert or Master	
World Wide Web	http://www.waves.com/	

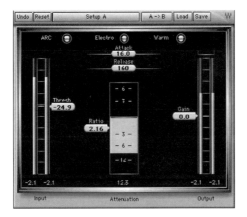

Concept

Renaissance Compressor, Rc if you're in a hurry, was the debut plug-in of the Waves Renaissance series. This package includes a mono and a stereo version. Unfortunately, the stereo version doesn't feature more sophisticated stuff like separate access to the individual channels or sidechain functions.

Actually, the concept of the entire plug follows along the same lines—it sticks to the basics and shuns the frills. The user interface is configured as three ›columns:‹

◆ INPUT: On the left side of the control panel, you'll see a large LED meter for the input level. At the bottom, the peak value is indicated in dB. You can reset this numeric display via a simple mouse click.

   With the THRESHOLD slider, which also displays numeric values in dB, you can determine the signal processing threshold directly by setting it to the desired value on the input level scale.

◆ ATTENUATION: At the center of the control panel, you'll find the RATIO slider. It is used to determine what happens to the signal when it exceeds the defined threshold, in other words, the degree of compression or expansion. Once a signal processing operation is underway, the adjacent column lights up to indicate as much.

◆ OUTPUT: The display for the output level is identical in form and function to the meter for the INPUT section. Numeric headroom indicators are also located at the bottom of this section of the panel.

All in all, pretty mundane stuff, but there's more to it then meets the eye—some sonic sleight of hand hidden in the algorithm. When the LED perched atop the level display illuminates red, this doesn't mean—as experience with just about any other level indicator might have taught you—that the plug-in's output signal is being tormented with digital distortion. Under these aurally dire circumstances, an integrated ›brickwall limiter‹ (see L1 from page 190 onwards) rears its welcome head. Thus the output level can never, ever exceed the critical 0-dB threshold, no matter how ill-advised a setting you happen to come up with.

At the top edge of the Rc box, you'll also find a couple of preset parameters. The faders for ATTACK (0.5 ms to 5 sec) and RELEASE (5 ms to 50 sec) let you determine how quickly the signal processing components respond when the signal rises above or dips below the THRESHOLD value.

ARC (›**A**uto **R**elease **C**ontrol‹) is a feature that is closely related to these parameters. If you care to, you can activate this function so that the release time that you determined is varied dynamically according to the audio material. This option is designed to minimize undesirable side effects and create a more natural sound.

The switch at the center lets you vary the response of the Rc. In ELECTRO mode, it reacts like greased lightning, which is just what the doctor ordered for drum loops and the like. OPTO is more laid back and gives you a softer ›vintage sound,‹ which is usually the right prescription for processing complex mixdowns.

Finally, WARM/SMOOTH lets you vary the fundamental sound of the compressor. As so often, let your ears be your guide.

Rating

With the Renaissance series, Waves evidently sought to compensate for the—at least in the eyes of the average Joe or Jane—extremely technical plugs such as the C1 compressor. Or maybe they just wanted to address a wider target group, move more units and go sailing for the rest of their days.

Anyway, the makers of the Renaissance plug-ins—like my editor—were obviously in the ›Let's get to the point, shall we?‹ frame of mind. These plugs were designed to offer only the essential parameters and thus be a piece of cake to handle. However, its author evidently also strove for a sound quality that at least comes close to doing justice to the discerning tastes of ›pros‹ and emulate the ›feel‹ of high-end analog devices.

What do you know, they actually did it, at least in the case of the Renaissance Compressor: its sound truly is very smooth and refined. What's more, its CPU demands are considerably lower those that of the C1. However, its interface must have been conceived under the glare of harshest neon. It's so dark that my first response was to look for its light switch, but that's more a matter of taste than a real gripe. The point is that even for newbies, it really is easy to suss.

All in all, the Rs Compressor is a good tip for users who are looking for expedient, uncomplicated means to get the job done and are willing to pass on frills and manual fine-tuning options.

The way the plug-in processes signals is unobtrusive, but nevertheless it polishes the sound very nicely. For furious signal mangling mania and out-there effects sounds, you'll have to look elsewhere. With its on-board limiter, the Renaissance Compressor also comes in real handy as a compact mastering plug-in.

The Renaissance Compressor will not be the last of its ilk. The Renaissance EQ is currently available and the company is apparently planning to introduce additional Renaissance plug-ins with a vintage feel and super-simple user interfaces.

Its only drawback is the relatively steep price. However, if you are willing and able to fork over the dough, I can't think of a single reason why I shouldn't recommend the Renaissance Compressor to you.

Tips & Tricks

To explore the mysteries of the RATIO sliders, you should first set the THRESH fader on the left to a relatively low value. Select a setting so that the signal level regularly exceeds this threshold.

◆ COMPRESSION: When you pull the RATIO fader from the neutral center position downwards, you are actually defining the compression: peak levels are attenuated depending on the setting (1:1.1 to a max. of 1:50). This is the normal Compressor mode.

◆ EXPANSION: When you push the RATIO slider upwards and exceed the 1:1 setting, you are making the plug generate something which in tech-talk is called ›expansion.‹

What's happening here is exactly the opposite of compression: peak levels are boosted even higher. The sonic gap between loud and quiet is actually being stretched, but the signal sounds quieter to our ears because it is less compact and thus, on the average, has less energy.

In contrast to compression, which is ubiquitous, expansion is an extraordinary dynamic processing option—it is rarely required in the real world. It does have its merits though, for example to correct the balance of levels between two signals that were irrevocably mixed together in an audio file. Another application option for an expander is ›reanimating‹ samples or loops that—in a bout of wild-eyed enthusiasm—were at some point overzealously compressed.

De-Essers

A de-esser is a special form of compressor. Here too, peak levels are attenuated, but only when they happen to reside in the lofty end of the frequency scale. One of the most common applications for a de-esser is processing the human voice:

Sibilance—those cobra-like ›sss‹ sounds—on tracks featuring speech and vocals often sound disproportionately loud. A de-esser lets you ›iron out‹ these kinks so that overall the track sounds more homogeneous.

A de-esser, like a compressor, doesn't really take anything away from a signal. And it certainly won't make your tracks sound dull or muddy. On the contrary, once you have dealt with sibilant sounds in say a vocal track, when you're EQing, you can give it more juice in the high end without emphasizing those irritating frequencies. The typical crystal-clear and at the same time velvety vocals that you have heard on some of the more high-end productions were usually made possible with the help of a de-esser.

SPL De-Esser

T

VST Windows	DirectX	✓
	VST PC	—
VST Macintosh	✓	
Available in VST Racks	Send Effects, Channel Inserts and Master	
Standard Routing	Insert or Master	
World Wide Web	http://www.steinberg.net/products/plugins.html	

Concept

SPL De-Esser is the plug-in edition of a 19" hardware device that has been a staple of many a studio for some time now.

Coping with its user interface couldn't be easier: First select whether you want to process a FEMALE or MALE voice. You can control the intensity of its signal processing power via the S-REDUCTION knob, the attenuation level is indicated dynamically in an LED chain.

The, believe it or not, final parameter is AUTO THRESHOLD, which lets you activate a function that automatically adjusts the input threshold value should you find this type of mechanism helpful.

The SPL crew is widely known for coming up with novel, refreshing ideas for peripheral devices. These are usually much-praised by studio rats for their ›musical‹ qualities. With the De-Esser plug-in, SPL did a good job of packing the hardware's attributes into a software product.

I don't want to get carried away with the details, but it's worth mentioning that the SPL De-Esser works along the lines of a totally unique principle. It does not simply squash sibilance in the manner of conventional compressors, it actually attenuates these ›s‹ sounds via phase shifting. What often happens when the treatment is too intense, the person doing the speaking or singing sounds just like the late great Liberace; in other words, you will hear a distinct lisp. Here, you can turn the processor S-REDUCTION knob up to extreme positions and your vocalist will still sound like he or she is singing rather than *th*inging.

For voice processing, there is currently no other plug-in that is as ›intelligent‹ and thus unobtrusive when you're treating tracks. If you're sure you want to de-es predominantly vocals, then SPL De-Esser is your best bet—definitely go for it.

If however you want to occasionally use a de-esser for more ›exotic‹ applications, for example to process complex mixdown material, then the SPL De-Esser is unsuitable. As good as it sounds, it doesn't give you enough manual tweaking options, so you'll be better off with the Waves DeEsser or C1.

Tips & Tricks

It's a good idea to activate the AUTO THRESHOLD function when the level of the input signal fluctuates considerably:

When you're dealing with an overly dynamic vocal track, conventional de-essers are problematic—you'll find it impossible to define a satisfactory threshold. If you set the threshold to too high a value, the sibilant sounds that occur in quieter passages escape processing. If on the other hand, you set too high a threshold, the de-esser treatment is over the top in the louder passages.

When you run into this type of problem, simply activate your trusty SPL De-Esser and then the AUTO THRESHOLD button—the algorithm will set the threshold automatically. Thus all dynamic stages get the same treatment, regardless of their levels.

Deactivating the AUTO THRESHOLD function only makes good sense if you want to ›push‹ the de-esser to extremes:

1 Load the plug to the SEND EFFECTS rack and route signals to it via SEND in PRE-fader mode with the channel fader pulled all the way down.

2 Try turning the channel's SEND knob and EFFECTS MASTER knob on the VST effects device input all the way up. Internally, the SPL De-Esser works with 32-bit floating point operations, so it has plenty of headroom. Actually, you'd be hard-pressed to saturate it internally.

3 Go to the De-Esser and turn the S-REDUCTION knob all the way up. Now switch the AUTO THRESHOLD button on and off. You will hear that the treatment is considerably more pronounced without AUTO THRESHOLD.

This is of course a deliberate effort at abusing the plug to create sound effects. For natural sounding, unobtrusive de-ess-

ing, you should use the De-Esser as an insert plug-in with
AUTO THRESHOLD mode activated.

Waves DeEsser

VST Windows	DirectX	✓
	VST PC	—
VST Macintosh	✓	
Available in VST Racks	Send Effects, Channel Inserts and Master	
Standard Routing	Insert or Master	
World Wide Web	http://www.waves.com/	

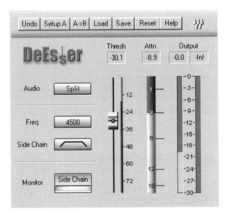

Concept

This de-esser plug-in is also dead-easy to handle. FREQ lets
you dial in the cutoff frequency. Below this feature, you can
select low- or band-pass filter characteristics.

Use the THRESH fader to determine the threshold level. The
current level of signal attenuation (ATTN) and the output level
(OUTPUT) are indicated via two large vertical LED meters.
That's about it for the key features.

There is one more option located at the left side of the control panel: AUDIO lets you determine if you want the entire

signal to be processed (WIDEBAND) or just the high end (SPLIT). In both cases, you can use MONITOR to hear only the filtered part of the signal, which actually controls the dynamic processing operation (SIDECHAIN).

Rating

The Waves DeEsser gives absolutely no cause for complaint. Handling is a breeze, all the crucial features are on board, and its sound does the trick for standard applications.

If however you already own the Waves C1, and equally importantly, know how to handle it, the Waves DeEsser would be redundant on your system. All the features of this plug-in are also part of the C1.

Actually, the C1 goes one better. It features an additional noise gate. This is a pretty handy little tool when used in combination with a de-esser—if you go for the Waves De-Esser, you'll have to do without it.

Evidently, the algorithms of the two plug-ins are close enough so that the differences are, at least to my ear, indistinguishable. If there really are audible divergences when you dial in standard settings to C1, it comes as news to me. The DeEsser however is less of a CPU hog, which considering that its functions were down-sized, isn't a huge surprise.

The bottom line is the Waves DeEsser is a conventional algorithm based on a standard compressor. What you're dealing with here is nothing more than an excerpt from the C1 range of functions presented on a similarly streamlined and thus substantially simpler interface.

Tips & Tricks

The interface of the DeEsser gives you just two options that are not entirely self-explanatory. One of these has to do with the correct status of the filter icon under SIDECHAIN:

◆ LOWPASS: Here the icon shows just a kink on its left-hand side. This is the standard mode in which the de-esser analyzes and processes all frequencies that lie above the cut-off frequency.

- ◆ BANDPASS: Here the icon shows a kind of tunnel shape. In Bandpass mode, only the frequency range surrounding the cutoff frequency play a role. You can give this mode a go in problematic situations where Lowpass mode is unable to deliver the desired sonic results. However, Bandpass mode was implemented half-heartedly—you can't change the filter quality, i.e. the width of the frequency ranges.

The other item has to do with how you go about selecting the right AUDIO option. If you read Tips & Tricks for the C1 and can recall what I was rambling about, you may actually recognize these terms:

- ◆ WIDEBAND: Only the selected frequency range is analyzed. When the threshold is exceeded, in this mode, the DeEsser not only attenuates the high frequencies, but the entire input signal.

Normally, a vocal track is going to have extremely few low frequencies at the point where sibilance is audible—its kind of hard to hiss in a baritone register, if you know what I mean. For standard vocal processing applications, you're better off selecting this mode. The results are generally less intrusive and more natural sounding.

The ›ideal‹ cutoff frequency for de-essing hasn't been identified yet and presumably never will—one man's trash is another's treasure. It of course depends on the material that you're dealing with. For male vocals, start with circa 4.5 to 5.5 kHz, for female vocals some 6 to 7 kHz and fine-tune from there.

- ◆ SIDECHAIN: Here, not only is just part of the signal analyzed, but solely the defined high-frequency range of the signal is attenuated. This mode is good for nailing say the overly dominant sizzle of a ride cymbal in a finished mixdown. The rest of the mixdown—i.e. all those nice warm bass and mids—can pass unharmed.

Combination Tools for Vocals

Many of the plug-ins discussed from here on out combine a number of disparate functions into a cohesive unit. The following were primarily designed for treating human voices.

Prosoniq VoxCiter

VST Windows	DirectX	—
	VST PC	(in the works)
VST Macintosh	✓	
Available in VST Racks	Send Effects, Channel Inserts and Master	
Standard Routing	Insert or Master	
World Wide Web	http://www.prosoniq.com/	

Concept

As its name claims, this is a combo tool designed for speech and vocals. The user interface is arranged in different sections that doggedly trace the signal path. From left to right, you'll find:

♦ IN: The ON button is nothing more than a BYPASS switch which lets you circumvent the entire plug. Kudos to its makers—way too many plug-ins don't give you this option.

♦ GATE: This is a noise gate used for suppressing stuff like rustling clothing, background noise or stalker-like heavy breathing audible when your hung-over vocalist gasps for air between lines. All the key parameters are on board. When the gate shuts shop, it doesn't kid around—it always closes down completely. Here you can't vary the ›noise floor,‹ a feature you won't miss for processing all but extremely noisy recordings.

◆ Eq 1: This is a fully parametric filter band featuring four variable characteristics (Low/High-Pass, Band-Cut/Reject).

◆ Compressor/Sidechain: Of all the sections, this is by far the most complex. The compressor features all the standard parameters. With the knob rotated hard left, you get a compression ratio of 25:1. When you turn the knob to the right, an ›e‹ appears next to the values indicating that the section is operating in Expander mode. This of course means that dynamics of the signal are enhanced rather than reduced.

In addition to fumbling with the Attack and Release times manually, you can use Auto to activate automatic program-dependent control of these parameters.

Rather than a separate section, the Sidechain segment at the bottom edge is another compressor mode that you can activate at will. Here you can filter the control signal for the compressor to narrow its effect down to a specific frequency range. The standard application for Sidechain/Compressor mode is de-essing, i.e. the search-and-destroy method of dealing with sibilants.

◆ Eq 2: It features the same doodads as Eq 1, except that here they are used to mangle the signal *after* it exits the compressor section.

◆ Drive: This is a simulation of an analog tape saturation effect similar to the one generated by the Steinberg/Spectral Design Magneto. In- and output levels and its characteristics are variable. The Bias knob at the left is equivalent to one found on an analog tape machine, the knob at the right gives you a response closer to that of a cranked tube amp.

♦ REFRESH: This is an enhancer section in which you can add overtones to the audio material for a more airy sound. Its parameters are:

DRIVE—intensity of the effect

SHAPE—rotated clockwise, it controls the balance between the first and second harmonics

TUNE—fundamental frequency of the added overtones

INTENSITY—output level of the effects signal

♦ OUTPUT—output levels

All sections can be activated separately, which not only affects the load on the CPU, it is also makes it much easier to dial in the desired effect step by step. The many integrated status LEDS and level meters are very helpful. This plug indicates if and how intense a signal processing stage is operating at every key point in the signal chain.

Rating

In contrast to most other Prosoniq plug-ins, the interface of the VoxCiter seems somewhat cluttered: a jam-packed gaggle of knobs, gloomy hard-to-read value scales and virtually indistinguishable section demarcations. Much to my amazement though, once you get used to it, you'll find the plug-in is pretty easy to handle—a condition favored by its generous array of status indicators and level meters.

At first glance, you may be irritated to find that the plug does not offer separate sections for the de-esser and compressor—you're always forced to choose between the two. But when you work with the plug for a while you'll see that the compressor section actually does a bang-up job of de-essing. What's more, you can run it as a de-esser and generate some compression via the DRIVE section.

All in all, VoxCiter is a somewhat unwieldy plug-in—some readers may take one look at its interface and, horrified at the perceived disarray, run. They'd be missing out. If you're looking for a comprehensive tool for making the most of vocal tracks and want a gadget featuring all the essential processing sections while using Cpu resources in relative moderation, then this is your plug.

Tips & Tricks

Again, the compressor section of the VoxCiter gives good de-essing, provided you dial in a suitable setup:

1 Patch VoxCiter into the mixer channel of a vocal track as an insert effect.

2 Use On at the far left to activate the entire plug-in, but switch on only one section, the Compressor in Sidechain mode (Compressor On, Sidechain On).

3 When you activate the Monitor option located at the bottom edge, you will hear the control signal of the compressor only. Try to isolate the sibilant sounds using the Sidechain knobs Gain, Frequency and Q.

4 Activate the De-ess option. The manual controls for the Sidechain filters are disabled and the algorithm locates sibilants all by its lonesome. All you will hear are the sibilant sounds. This tells us that the algorithm truly is ›intelligent.‹

5 Switch Monitor off. You will hear the de-esser at work. Activate Auto, vary the Threshold and use Ratio (knob to the left) to control the intensity of the effect.

To generate the *ersatz* compression mentioned earlier, all you have to do is go to the Drive section and turn In Gain well up. Be sure to keep an eye on the Overload Led! Turn Out Gain down accordingly and rotate Bias counter-clockwise towards –99.

The signal sounds warmer, more compact and direct without actually being saturated. If you want distortion, experiment with Bias values located in the Pm range (after 12 o'clock) of the knob.

Waves AudioTrack

VST Windows	DirectX	✓
	VST PC	—
VST Macintosh	✓	
Available in VST Racks	Send Effects, Channel Inserts and Master	
Standard Routing	Insert or Master	
World Wide Web	http://www.waves.com/	

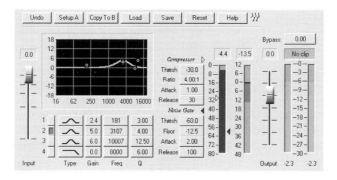

Concept

AudioTrack is an amalgam of a 4-band EQ, compressor and gate. The algorithms, user interface and concept of the individual sections are equivalent to those of the separately available plugs-ins Q10 and C1, but here the features and functions are streamlined editions of the fully-loaded versions:

◆ EQ: The filter is equivalent to a Q4, i.e. a Q10 with four fully parametric bands. The only other concession here is the somewhat smaller frequency response display, everything else is cloned from big brother.

◆ COMPRESSOR: Its algorithm was copped from the C1 Compressor, but you'll have to settle for a bar display only—there's no graphical indication of what the dynamic response curve is up to. In terms of variable parameters, you get THRESHOLD, RATIO (0.5:1 to 40:1), ATTACK and RELEASE. A closer look at the RATIO parameter would tell you that the control range is not quite as extensive as on the C1.

♦ GATE: Same as above—identical to the C1 Gate except without a display for the characteristic curve. The parameters are THRESHOLD, FLOOR, ATTACK and RELEASE. You won't find an Expander mode nor separate GATE OPEN and GATE CLOSE parameters.

Finally, AudioTrack comes complete with an input and output level control section with a dedicated display.

Rating

AudioTrack is a fair compromise for everyone who doesn't want to go whole hog and invest in the entire Waves Native Power Pack with Q10 and C1. Particularly its compressor and gate sections are limited to the ›classic‹ functions and displays. Although you won't be able to knock out several special applications with this tool, it gives you what you need to deal with all standard applications. Plus handling is less technically oriented, thus much easier.

Then there's the fact that an AudioTrack plug-in demands appreciably less CPU resources then a combination of Q4 and C1. Finally, the three processors are already set up in a serial circuit, which will suit most users just fine.

Tips & Tricks

The AudioTrack seems predestined for voice processing. The only function that is missing—in comparison to a classic voice processor—is a de-esser, everything else is on board:

1   Plug AudioTrack as an INSERT effect into a vocal track.

2   Select the AudioTrack preset ›Voice with presence‹ as the template for processing the voice.

3 Deactivate the compressor and gate. Since AudioTrack isn't equipped with separate bypass buttons for this purpose, deactivate the compressor by turning the COMPRESSOR THRESHOLD parameter all the way up to 0, the gate by turning the GATE THRESHOLD parameter down to $-\infty$.

4 Fuss with the EQ parameters to find the best setting and once you're finished, activate the compressor and maximize its parameters.

5 Finally, activate the gate and dial in the settings that sound best.

6 Save the plug-in's current setup as a preset and give it the name of the vocalist. This way when at some point you want to process another track featuring this person's voice—be it spoken or sung—all you have to is load the preset!

Finally, here are two more tips that may come in handy when you're working with AudioTrack:

◆ Ignore the parameter Bp located at the top edge of the control panel. It has no function in VST.

◆ Note that depending on the relative settings of the EQ and compressor or compressor and gate, you may encounter digital saturation and thus audible distortion.

AudioTrack is not equipped with any kind of level meters or displays that enable you to visually monitor these ›junctions‹ in the signal circuit. In other words, you may hear distortion, but you certainly won't be able to see it. You'll simply have to trust your ears!

Pitch Correction

Although the range of available VST-compatible plug-ins for every other type of effect boggles the mind, pitch manipulation tools are rather rare beasts. No reason to cry though because the following two plugs are real winners, each in its own way.

Antares Auto Tune VST

VST Windows	DirectX	✓
	VST PC	—
VST Macintosh	✓	
Available in VST Racks	Send Effects and Channel Inserts	
Standard Routing	Insert or Master	
World Wide Web	http://www.antares-systems.com/	

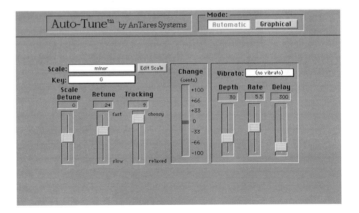

Concept

Auto-Tune analyzes a monophonic input signal, compares the frequencies of notes with an ›ideal‹ tuning for the given key and, if necessary, corrects the pitch. Ideally, this means that you could pipe in Lou Reed-ish vocals and something that sounds like Mariah Carey will come out the other end. Sort of.

The plug-in features two modes that are not only totally disparate in concept, but also feature dissimilar interfaces:

Automatic Mode

First you have to tell the plug what key your song is in via SCALE/KEY. SCALE DETUNE gives you a fine-tuning option should your song deviate from the ›official‹ concert pitch of A. For each note of a scale, you can even determine if it is muted entirely or exempted from pitch correction (EDIT SCALE).

In Auto Tune, Automatic is the normal mode for minor corrections. It works in realtime.

RETUNE lets you determine how fast the pitch is corrected. TRACKING defines how far a note has to deviate from the ideal pitch before it is corrected. The CHANGE bar gives you a visual indication of how intense the material is being processed.

At the right of the control panel, you'll find three parameters that let you add an ›artificial‹ vibrato if this happens to ring your bell. Of course this vibrato sounds a bit too even and thus unnatural, so don't expect to pipe in your average Brit-popper and have Aaron Neville come out the other end.

Graphical Mode

Resort to this mode only when you are unable to come up with satisfactory results using AUTOMATIC. This is usually the case if some of the notes you are routing into the plug-in input are more than a quarter note off. Then of course Auto-Tune is ineffective—it can't figure out where it is that you wanted to go.

In GRAPHICAL mode, you have the option of analyzing the audio material and viewing the pitch deviations in a graphical display. You can then either have the program compute corrections and edit this curve manually or draw a completely new pitch curve.

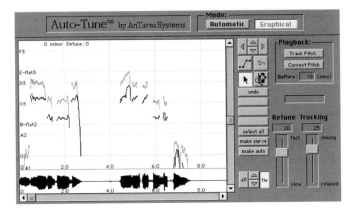

Pitches are then corrected according to this template curve, whereby the intensity and rate of the correction can be varied globally via the Tracking and Retune faders.

Rating

Auto Tune debuted for the platform ProTools Tdm and caused quite a stir when it did. The fact that it is now even available as a separate box tells us that enough people liked it well enough to warrant the production of a stand-alone hardware device. The good news is that although this is a high-end algorithm, you won't be able to take home at a lower price than in the Vst version.

The audio quality of this plug-in is—I'll make no bones about it—excellent. You won't be impressed if you try to transpose vocal lines by several semitones, but then this is not what the plug-in was designed for. If the pitch correction that you're attempting is within reason and the parameters are tweaked to the ideal settings, the plug will not produce any audible side effects.

The only reservation I have is a minor one: Graphical mode requires that you invest some time in getting the hang of it. If you're willing to put in a few extra hours and a tool like Auto Tune is suitable for your audio material, I can recommend this plug-in without reservations.

Tips & Tricks

Whereas AUTOMATIC mode is child's play in terms of handling, you'll have to put in some effort to acquire the requisite skills for GRAPHICAL mode. This is certainly not because its concept or implementation is flawed, it's just that—like many of the more enjoyable things in life—it takes some practice to get proficient. Here's the best way to get started:

1 In the VST ARRANGEMENT, set the LEFT marker to the start of the material that you want to correct. This is very important because you must be able to start playback several times from precisely the same position.

2 Set the VST song cursor to the Left Locator by pressing ⑦ on the numeric key pad.

3 In Auto Tune, select AUTOMATIC mode and enter the key that the audio material you are planning on editing is in.

4 Now activate GRAPHICAL mode and prepare Auto Tune to analyze your stuff by clicking on the TRACK PITCH button.

5 Start playback in VST. Hit STOP as soon as the passage you want to fix has run through to the end.

6 Auto Tune just analyzed the audio signal. At the bottom edge of the window, you'll see a graphical representation of the material's waveform and at the top, a red curve that depicts pitch deviations as the occur in the passage.

7 Although you shouldn't do it just now, when you click on the MAKE CURVE button, Auto Tune will do just that, draw a black curve that is equivalent to the red curve. This curve will come in handy when you want to fine-tune the treatment manually.

8 Instead, click on the MAKE AUTO button. The Auto Tune plug now interprets the material and computes an ›ideal‹ curve that has already been corrected. At every point where the red and black curves deviate, the plug corrected the pitch.

9 Set the VST song cursor to the start position. In Auto-Tune, click on the CORRECT PITCH button and activate play in VST. Now you will hear the results of the pitch correction.

This is the initial procedure in GRAPHICAL mode. Up to this point, the results of the described processing are identical to what AUTOMATIC mode will produce.

The appeal of GRAPHICAL mode is that you can edit the black curve that the plug generated via the MAKE CURVE button like you would in a drawing program. Here's a quick look at the most important methods:

◆ Select the arrow tool and draw a box around a continuous segment of the black curve. You'll see two ›handles.‹

  If you move just one of the handles, you will bend the curve accordingly. This lets you compensate when the vocalist didn't quite hit the desired note in a phrase.

  If you select the start and end handle of a phrase while holding the ⌂ key down, you can move the entire phrase, for instance to transpose an individual syllable.

▶ When you're editing in this manner, you will generally want the target point to have a different vertical position while the horizontal position remains intact. For this purpose, press and hold the 𝑎𝑙𝑡 key when you're moving points.

◆ ›Optimizing‹ the black curve is not the only option for getting the job done. You can use the drawing tools—these are the two symbols located under the cursor buttons—to sketch your own curves. For example, you can continually drop the pitch of a sustained note.

▶ Please keep in mind that you can't ›stack‹ several curves here. There can only be one curve segment at any given time for a given phrase. It determines the pitch. If you draw a new segment at this position, you will delete whatever you drew or was generated by the program earlier for this particular point on the curve.

Finally, you should use track bouncing to load the results to an audio file. Whereas for AUTOMATIC mode, this is ›just‹ a really sensible thing to do, it is mandatory for GRAPHICAL mode! In this aspect, Auto-Tune truly is unique among VST plug-ins.

Steinberg/Spectral Design Ultravox

Vst Windows	DirectX	—
	Vst Pc	✓
Vst Macintosh	✓	
Available in Vst Racks	Send Effects, Channel Inserts and Master	
Standard Routing	Insert	
World Wide Web	http://www.spectral-design.com/	

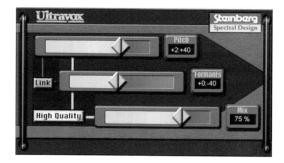

Concept

Ultravox is a pitch shifter, i.e. a plug-in that lets you manipulate the pitch of an audio signal. Although the plug looks pretty nondescript, don't underestimate it. Two of its features are unquestionably impressive:

◆ REALTIME: Ultravox does its thing instantaneously. Granted, all other Vst plug-ins are realtime-capable, but it is worth mentioning here because the majority of pitch shift algorithms aren't.

◆ FORMANT SHIFTING: The plug-in enables separate access to pitch and formant shifting processes.

Formant shifting requires some explanation: Every natural or acoustic sound has specific, very distinct frequency ranges, so-called ›formants.‹ For example when a vocalist sings different notes, the fundamental pitch changes but the formant frequencies more or less stay the same. Like an ›acoustic fingerprint‹ these frequencies are primarily responsible for shaping the timbre of a voice, making each one unique.

Less sophisticated pitch shift algorithms take the entire signal and shift all frequencies contained therein by the same measure. It doesn't exempt the formants from processing, so when you transpose a vocal recording downwards, the vocalist sounds like Lurch on valium and transposed upwards, Minnie Mouse on helium.

Ultravox identifies formant frequencies and is able to segregate these from other frequencies, as you can see when you take a closer look at the two faders on the user interface:

◆ PITCH: Here you can manipulate the pitch within a range of one octave up and down. If you work with just this fader, the formants are not influenced and the transposition largely sounds very natural, depending on how far a leap you are contemplating.

◆ FORMANTS: Here you can control formant shifting, i.e. manipulate the characteristics of a voice, independently of pitch.

If you want to create a standard pitch shifter sound, all you have to do is punch the LINK button. Then the formant frequencies are shifted automatically when you move the PITCH fader. The results sound relatively unnatural, but this can be desirable for some productions.

Apart from these control features, the only other components you'll find on the plug-in interface are a MIX fader, which lets you determine the balance of the input and effects signals, and a HIGH QUALITY button. This may not come as a revelation, but only when this button is activated does the Ultravox deliver the best possible effects quality. This of course demands a tribute in terms of more CPU resources. If you can somehow manage to coax the requisite horsepower from your computer, do it—it's well worth it.

Rating

Ultravox is a truly spectacular effect. In HIGH QUALITY mode, which requires about the same amount of CPU power as Waves TrueVerb, you can manipulate pitch up to a range of some five to six semitone steps while retaining a relatively natural sound.

Don't expect it to do ridiculous stuff like a lead vocal track by a fifth and expect it to sound peachy keen. But so what—if a track requires this radical a treatment, the reasoning behind it was flawed to begin with. Slight corrections of lead tracks by one to two semitone steps are entirely feasible, as are the greater intervals mentioned previously for background harmonies.

There are pitch shifters out there that do a better job of delivering more natural sound for transpositions over greater intervals. Unlike the Ultravox, these generally don't do their thing in realtime and can't match the excellence of its formant shifting feature—if they even offer something similar at all.

You could say this feature is the star of the plug's sonic show. It will even let you conjure up some real audio magic. For example, if you're working with a recording of a female vocalist who has all the blue-eyed soul of say a Spice Girl, Ultravox will let you add a pinch of Aretha Franklin: simply turn the FORMANTS fader down for a touch of ›gospel.‹

If you take this to extremes, the voice will cross the gender line. You can use the same female vocal track to come up with a number of male voices with different timbres, all unique and relatively natural sounding. This feature is great for conjuring up backing vocals featuring male and female harmonists from a single vocal track which, unlike the usual pitch shifter treatments, sounds very vital and natural.

Tips & Tricks

When you're processing voices, if you mess with the PITCH fader only and leave the FORMANTS fader in the neutral center position, you won't come up with the most natural-sounding results. What seems to do the trick in many cases is to move the FORMANTS fader a tad in the opposite direction of the PITCH fader—when you're transposing upwards, back the FORMANTS fader off a hair to set a negative value and vice versa.

If you used Ultravox solely for ›natural‹ transpositions, you'd be missing half the fun. Try to ›pump up‹ or ›shrink‹ a piano sound via the FORMANTS.

Although the distinction may minor, you can also use the plug-in as an effect rather than a processor:

1 Plug Ultravox into a drum loop track as an insert effect.

2 Set MIX to 100% and select an extreme PITCH value, e.g. +12.

3 Experiment with the FORMANTS fader by sweeping it through its entire value range. If you switch HIGH QUALITY mode off, you can come up with even more radical effects.

▶ If you want to use Ultravox to turn a vocal track into a set of backing harmonies, plug it in as an insert effect, set MIX to 100%, set the remaining parameters as desired and record the results via track bouncing. Repeat this procedure until you have come up with enough voices.

Once you have generated these audio regions, in VST ARRANGE, set them up in parallel on different tracks, cut the regions by syllables and mute the regions that don't sound right until you like what you're hearing. That's all it takes to come up with your very own homegrown ›Bohemian Rhapsody.‹

Vintage and Retro Effects

For years, we implored the audio gods to bestow upon us the miracle of digital technology because it crackles, pops and hisses much less than its analog counterpart. After our prayers were answered, many of us lusted for plug-ins that nostalgically revive that ›vintage feel.‹ Well, now that intrepid programmers came up with just the kind of plugs that will add some dirt, there's good news and bad news: If you're a VST Windows user, you can satisfy at least some of the craving for a funkier sound with the Grungelizer, but if you're a Macintosh disciple, nada. You'll have to venture forth armed with a credit card to hunt for something that you can load to your plug-in rack.

Steinberg/Spectral Design Magneto

VST Windows	DirectX	✓
	VST PC	(in the works)
VST Macintosh	✓	
Available in VST Racks	Send Effects, Channel Inserts and Master	
Standard Routing	Insert or Master	
World Wide Web	http://www.spectral-design.com/	

Concept

Magneto was designed to simulate one of the more (in)famous side effects of analog tape recordings—so-called ›tape saturation.‹ This effect was presumably ›discovered‹ when engineers, in an attempt to get the loudest possible recordings, turned up the levels to a point near tape saturation. Later, many found this effect desirable—some studio maestros even saturated tapes *on purpose*.

When you're working with analog gear—digital equipment won't do—this achieves a complex combination of frequency-dependent distortion and compression. Tape saturation is often used to make drums or basses sound ›fatter.‹

Magneto's user interface was inspired by the historic gear it was modeled on—its visuals are all vintage Vu level meters and knobs. Next to the in- and output levels, Tape Speed and a high frequency control (Hf-Adjust), Drive is by far the most important parameter.

It lets you determine how high a level you are ›recording‹ to the virtual analog tape. This level in turn influences the degree of generated compression and distortion.

Although Magneto can be loaded to the Master Effects rack, I would in most cases not recommend using it to compress the master signal. Undesirable side effects such as a dreaded ›pumping‹ sound simply happen too soon and often—especially since it doesn't feature a Link parameter allowing you to marry the two stereo channels.

To monitor the simulation visually, all you have to do is set the buttons at the top edge to determine if the Vu meters indicate the in- or output levels, or the level of the virtual analog tape.

Rating

Magneto does an excellent job of what it was designed to do. The simulated analog tape saturation effects sound very good and—depending on the type of material you're working with—can certainly add considerably more punch, warmth and complexity to digital recordings.

Its appetite for Cpu resources is roughly comparable to that of the Waves TrueVerb, which is of course relatively healthy. You'll need at a least a mid-class computer to run this plug-in.

Magneto is combination consisting of a ›retro‹ effect and compressor, so you could theoretically use this plug in place of any ›normal‹ compressor. However, you should keep in mind that when you process complex signals with this plug, its treatment won't be nearly as unobtrusive as that of a limiter or multiband compressor designed specifically to maximize the loudness of master signals.

Tips & Tricks

Magneto is great for processing just certain parts of your audio mixdowns rather than the entire master signal. In my experience, it sounds amazing when applied to drum loops, basses or guitars. If you crank the DRIVE parameter to the hilt, you can generate a relatively conspicuous dose of distortion. Although it may not spare you and your neighbors the full sonic onslaught of a Marshall stack when you're trying to lay down screaming lead tracks, it will add some bluesy dirt to electric guitars recorded directly to the console.

If you dial in more subtle settings, you can even use Magneto for vocal tracks. Start with a DRIVE setting no higher than +10 dB and a TAPE SPEED of 30 ips for a kind of breathy sound. Tweak HF-ADJUST to boost the high end a touch.

This setup produces something akin to an analog exciter sound, which treats vocals so that they sound more airy and livelier than the usual treble boost via EQ.

Opcode fusion:Vinyl

VST Windows	DirectX	✓
	VST PC	(in the works)
VST Macintosh		(in the works)
Available in VST Racks		Send Effects, Channel Inserts and Master
Standard Routing		Insert or Master
World Wide Web		`http://www.opcode.com/products/ fusioneffects`

Concept

Vinyl takes you way back to the wonderful world of crackling LPs and skipping styluses. The plug-in simulates the detrimental influences of vinyl pressing processes, aging and wear as well as the inherent limitations of turntables.

The most important features for turning your virtual LPs into relics from a bygone age are located in the RECORD SURFACE section. If you prefer, you can have the plug do the work for you—simply select one of the predefined conditions, from a brand new, high-end import (VIRGIN PLAY) to something that sounds like it was used as a coaster for countless pitchers of beer (WORN OUT). Or if you are the tinkering type, you can also fuss with each parameter individually:

◆ DIRT: Adds general funk to the surface, primarily in the form of mid-range crackle.

◆ STATIC: You remember static charges on your beloved LPs—this coats tracks with a sheen of delicate high-frequency crackle.

◆ HISS: Yesssssss.

◆ WEAR: Did you ever love a particular track so much that you played it thousands of times over the years? That's what you get—very realistic distortion.

◆ SCRATCHES: Amount and level of scratches. A more realistic scale would have been something that describes the aftermath of your average teenage soiree—from Dismal Gathering (very few, very slight scratches) to Excellent Bash (virtually unplayable). Speaking of realism, in contrast to the other very convincing crackling effects, if you're a stickler for authenticity, here you can discern a distinctly artificial pattern to the scratches.

◆ WARP: In the graphic on the Vinyl's interface, you can play with the ›warp factor‹ by bending the virtual LP via the vertical fader. This messes with the pitch to create a seasick kind of wobbly effect.

◆ FADE OUT: Normally, the warp in a vinyl platter is more pronounced on the outer rim. If you play a side all the way through, it will sound more wobbly at the beginning than towards the end. This is what FADE OUT simulates, the pertinent question however is who really needs it?

The TURNTABLE/SYSTEM section deals with the influences that different sound systems can have. Here too, you get five presets for the lazy and separately editable parameters for the more industrious:

◆ BANDWIDTH: This is a band-pass filter that lets you limit the frequencies of the signal to any range you see fit. This gives you a sound dominated by mids, making the track sound less hi-fi, more like a kazoo played through a foghorn.

◆ ST WIDTH: Similar to BANDWITH, except that it squeezes the stereo spread. Here you can seamlessly sweep the signal towards mono.

◆ COMPRESS: A simple compressor that squashes the dynamics by a variable measure.

◆ SPEED: These three buttons let you select how fast the virtual turntable spins—33, 45 or 78 RPM.

◆ RUMBLE: For that infamous turntable patter, with variable level.

These sections operate largely independently of one another. Ergo you can freely combine the two types of treatment options or when appropriate, use just one of the sections and disregard the other entirely.

Rating

Sure, VST Windows users have the Grungelizer at their disposal, but its processing possibilities don't even come close to comparing with those of the Vinyl. I recommend this plugin to all who enjoy dabbling with retro/vintage sounds. If you want your recordings to crackle like someone is frying a herd of live pigs next door, this is a dream come true. For creating truly damaged sounds, I know of no other plug that can compare.

The parameters give you highly detailed destructo options—everything you need to run signals through the lo-fi wringer is on board. This of course gives you a vast range of effects to choose from. Not only can you come up with thousands of variations on vinyl crackle, but you can also compress and add slight distortion to audio material. All treatments sound very dynamic and realistic.

Unfortunately, in terms of performance, Vinyl Version 1.0 followed all too closely in the footsteps of the CPU killer fusion:Vocode. With Version 1.1, the situation has improved markedly. Today Vinyl roughly requires the same amount of juice as a Waves Q8. You will be able to run this plug-in on a mid-class PC. If however your computer is already struggling, you should refrain from attempting all too ambitious parameter changes during playback. Apart from that, Vinyl is a really well-behaved little plug.

Tips & Tricks

Some parameters interact in a manner that is not immediately apparent just by glancing at the interface of Vinyl:

◆ The red arrow next to the RECORD SURFACE pop-up menu lets you determine if a preset that you have loaded includes SCRATCHES or not. In other words, do you want hear scratches that are generated automatically?

◆ The SPEED parameter not only influences RUMBLE, but also some other parameters such as WARP and SCRATCHES even though it is physically located in the TURNTABLE section.

When you're working with the Vinyl, try showing some blatant disregard for its primary purpose and see if you can't abuse it for other stuff: For example, set all parameters to neutral values and experiment with different combinations of WEAR and COMPRESS only.

This type of setup lets you treat guitars, basses, drums and percussion loops, samples or anything else that sounds too clean to your ears with a very special kind of aural funk: Sounds are compressed, they become somewhat more inarticulate and the bottom end tends to bubble in the background, ever so slightly lagging behind the rest of the signal. This lets you contrive exquisitely sloppy retro grooves—without adding crackle to the mix.

Stereo Manipulations

If you do your own mixdowns, it's up to you to distribute the different dry and wet signals throughout the stereoscape for maximum effect. Generally, you will only need special tools that allow you to manipulate the stereo attributes if you want to redress shortcomings in a near finalized stereo mixdown where for whatever reason you no longer have access to individual tracks.

Waves S1

VST Windows	DirectX	✓
	VST Pc	—
VST Macintosh	✓	
Available in VST Racks	Send Effects, Channel Inserts and Master	
Standard Routing	Insert or Master	
World Wide Web	http://www.waves.com/	

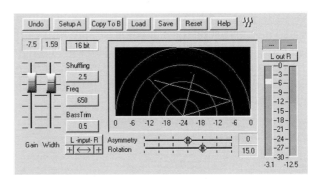

Concept

S1 is a typical mastering application. The plug-in sports every conceivable option for manipulating aspects relevant to the stereo image. You can choose from four plug-in versions:

◆ S1: The ›main plug-in‹ with integrated IDR (see page 192).

- S1 SHUFFLER: Same, but without IDR.

- S1 STEREO IMAGER: A leaner version of the S1 Shuffler sans the SHUFFLING, FREQUENCY and BASSTRIM parameters.

- S1 MS: A simple decoder lacking any parameters whatsoever. It is designed to work with recordings featuring middle/side micing, a special type of stereo signal that is no longer particularly en vogue.

The plug gives you a visual indication of what's going on via a display featuring concentric semicircles. The semicircle furthest from the center represents the peak digital level (0 dBFS); the level decreases as the ›orbit‹ moves closer to the center.

At the center of the semicircles, you'll find an isosceles triangle. The top horizontal side represents the width of the stereo image. The way the triangle is aligned indicates the stereo balance.

At the plug-in's signal input, you have the options of swapping the right and left stereo channels, rotating phases separately or launching a mid/side decoding operation. The following parameters are mirrored in the graphical display:

- GAIN: Controls the overall level represented by the height of the triangle.

- WIDTH: Controls the breadth of the stereo image represented by the width of the top side of the triangle.

- ROTATION: Here the triangle is tipped to one side. The subjective perception of the balance of levels within a mix remains intact while the absolute balance of levels between the left and right channels changes.

- ASYMMETRY: Here the triangle seemingly turns on its axis towards the observer. Acoustically, the result is that the subjective perception of the balance of levels between the left and right channels changes. Signals positioned at the center of the stereoscape are not influenced and the level balance between stereo channels remains largely constant.

Then there's the so-called SHUFFLING function, which is not mirrored in the graphic because its effect is frequency-dependent. Here you can—within a reasonable range—expand the stereo width of the bottom end. This counteracts a particular physical phenomenon—the somewhat flawed spacial perception of human hearing. Our ears find it difficult to localize low frequencies, which is why we perceive them as being more centered or tighter than the rest of a mixdown.

You can vary the cutoff frequency below which the effect kicks in (FREQUENCY: 350 Hz to 1.4 kHz) and the effects intensity (SHUFFLING).

Plus you get a BASS TRIM parameter that allows you control bass signals globally.

Rating

S1 is closer to a tool than an effect, by which I mean that the manipulation options work in a more traditional vein. On the downside, this means that you can't use it to generate impressive effects such as 3D sound modeling, pseudo stereo or auto panning.

On the upside, the S1 algorithms don't produce undesirable side effects such as diminished mono compatibility, provided you use them conscientiously and selectively.

Ergo if you occasionally find yourself restoring or maximizing finished mixdowns, the S1 can help you out of a bind.

If something is awry with the stereo balance of the material—for example the stereo image is too tight, there's a hole at the center of the stereoscape or your subjective perception of the balance gives you a bad vibe even if everything looks just fine on the level meters—S1 will help you fix the mix without adverse side effects.

Tips & Tricks

Whereas the majority of S1 parameters are easy to understand and handle, two—ASYMMETRY and ROTATION—are at least initially perplexing. Presumably this is because there's nothing truly comparable out there in the real world when you're doing hands-on mixing at a hardware console.

Your best bet is to take it slow and listen closely to what type of aural response you get when you change these parameters. You'll find it will take some experience to make the most of these features. On the other hand, some users may never need these relatively complex mechanisms.

When you begin exploring the plug, click on the space between the ASYMMETRY and ROTATION faders. This selects both faders—they're linked so that you can move them simultaneously. Although the S1 does not come with a dedicated knob for stereo balance, when you're moving the two faders in tandem, this is exactly what you end up with—a classic stereo balance control that in many cases will already give you a satisfactory correction. Plus the process is a heck of a lot easier to understand than manipulating signals separately via ASYMMETRY and ROTATION.

De-Noisers and De-Clickers

In this section, we'll take a break from the more spectacular effects and look at a breed of plugs that don't actually do all that much. However, it is crucial that what they do, they do as well and unobtrusively as possible. These are designed to eliminate undesirable noise and paradoxically sound best when you can't hear them do their thing.

Thanks to the digital revolution, noise is not nearly the problem it was some years ago. However, any number of components—mixing consoles, microphones, sound generators, A/D convertors *ad infinitum* can add to the noise level. Despite being perceived as antiseptic, even when working in the digital realm, you can end up with a dense fog of noise that clouds your entire mix.

On the other hand, removing clicks is important primarily when you are processing material from vinyl records. But even in conventional mixing situations, this type of tool can come in handy to eradicate an annoying acoustic pulse or a digital dropout on a track that you know the vocalist will never again be able to nail as well as on this flawed take. In these types of scenarios, you may be overjoyed to own a special plug-in that otherwise rarely sees any use.

⊚ T   Steinberg/Spectral Design DeNoiser

VST Windows	DirectX	✓
	VST PC	—
VST Macintosh	✓	
Available in VST Racks	Send Effects, Channel Inserts and Master	
Standard Routing	Insert or Master	
World Wide Web	`http://spectral-design.com/`	

Concept

When you feed a signal to this plug-in, it analyzes the noise floor and displays it dynamically as a green frequency spectrum. The REDUCTION fader lets you define the degree of de-noising.

With the LEVEL fader, you can determine the threshold of the algorithm. In the display, it is depicted as a yellow line. Once this line reaches the level of the noise floor, the line wraps itself around it, shaping something akin to a dynamic filter band. Under NOISEFLOOR, the plug-in displays the average level of the noise floor it has calculated.

You can of course turn the threshold (LEVEL) up higher than the displayed noise floor. Keep in mind though that the *higher* the green line in the display, the *lower* the threshold.

This however doesn't change the yellow filter curve, the displayed NOISEFLOOR or the aural effect of the plug's noise suppression. DeNoiser automatically prevents you from going overboard when you're trying to filter out noise.

The final signal-shaping parameter is AMBIENCE. It lets you fiddle with the balance of the original signal and the de-noised signal. If the treatment ends up sounding too sterile to your ears, you can dial in higher AMBIENCE values to roughen up the edges of the signal. Keep in mind though that the higher you turn up AMBIENCE, the more noise you will add to the mix, which may be kind of counterproductive since this is a de-noiser.

Rating
Some users prefer to work with de-noisers that can analyze certain ›noise prints,‹ save this unique spectrum and use it later as the template for processing other signal. Although

the DeNoiser works with these noise prints, you can't save and archive a noise spectrum.

If you can live without this feature, you'll find that this plug-in is a handy tool, just what the doctor ordered for most users. The quality of the algorithm is very good, and both graphical support and handling are fine as far as I'm concerned.

Tips & Tricks

Particularly for a de-noiser plug-in, a bypass is essential. It lets you check if the treatment is trampling all over high-end frequencies, a scenario which most users will find intolerable. In VST, the DeNoiser does not have a dedicated Bypass button, but you can rig one using the temporary A/B memory slots located at the right edge of the plug-in:

1 Before you start processing, set all three DeNoiser faders to 0 (LEVEL and AMBIENCE down, REDUCTION up).

2 Click on STORE and then B. Now you have captured a neutral setting where the plug-in does not influence the signal and loaded it to the temporary B memory.

3 Set the parameters as desired.

4 Whenever you want to compare the original and processed signals via this bogus bypass, click on STORE A to save the current setting to memory A. Click on B to call up the neutral setting—the fake bypass—and on A for the processed signal.

5 You can edit the parameters to your heart's content in A. Whenever you want to compare whatever you came up to what it was before you got started, then repeat Step 4 to do the bypass thing.

▶ Like virtually all plug-ins that analyze audio material, DeNoiser requires a moment or two to x-ray the audio material—here somewhere in the vicinity of a second—before it can move on to bigger and better things. So before you ›officially‹ process a signal, you should let the plug-in place a short snippet of the audio material under its virtual microscope.

When you play a brief sequence back, the DeNoiser commits the results of the analysis to memory (›noise print‹). The next time you start playback, it has the data it needs to get to work immediately.

Steinberg/Spectral Design DeClicker

VST Windows	DirectX	✓
	VST PC	—
VST Macintosh		✓
Available in VST Racks	Send Effects, Channel Inserts and Master	
Standard Routing	Insert or Master	
World Wide Web	http://spectral-design.com/	

Concept

This plug-in is designed to automatically purge ›impurities‹ from audio material and restore the spots at which they occurred so that the meddlesome noises are no longer audible. The plug features four areas on its control panel that let you set it up for the type of audio material you plan on dealing with:

◆ MODE: Here you can chose from

OLD—processing historic material,
STANDARD—universal, and
MODERN—processing contemporary productions with a relatively broad bandwidth or if you prefer, loads of high end.

For ›normal‹ de-click-
ing, you should al-
ways set this para-
meter to OFF so that
the signal remains as
pristine as possible.

- THRESHOLD: This fader lets you define the threshold at which the plug identifies clicks.

- DE-PLOP: When you push this fader upwards, the algorithm not only tracks down high frequency noise pulses, but also checks for mid-range pops. For example, this feature can help nail those pesky microphone plops.

- CLICK REDUCTION: In the bottom section of the plug, you can select four stages between the two extremes QUANTITY and QUALITY. Here you're telling the plug that you want it to do a search-and-destroy number on a bunch of clicks located close together or prefer it to work more subtly to produce the highest quality restoration that it can muster.

The AUDITION button lets you listen to the clicks that it found individually. Alongside this aural control feature, you get visual aids that help you come up with the right parameter settings, the following two displays:

In the top display, DSP PERFORMANCE, a curve continuously indicates the plug-in's load. If the curve hits the upper edge, these means that algorithm is at this moment unable to register all clicks or can no longer restore these properly.

In the bottom window, DECLICK PERFORMANCE, the plug continually draws a graphical representation of the input signals—you'll see a green waveform. If it detects something that shouldn't be there and processes it, this spot is marked. In theory a good idea, but it's kind of hard to see, so in practice it won't be of much help to you.

Rating

First the bad news: DeClicker is not very good at ›de-crack-ling‹ an incessant blanket of noise like the kind found on vintage vinyl, but then again this is not what it was designed for.

The plug does a much better job when it is tasked with ousting individual clicks that don't lie too close together. It usually manages to identify these just fine, but doesn't always eliminate them entirely. You may occasionally find yourself having to repeat the treatment.

If you're willing to go this extra mile, DeClicker will generally reward you by fixing clicks and drop-outs relatively satisfactorily. However, this plug-in is by no means a ›fail-safe‹ tool. To accurately be able to distinguish between undesirable clicks and original peak pulses in signals, it definitely needs a couple of more IQ points worth of ›artificial intelligence.‹ Go for this plug-in only if you can live with the fact that it will remedy some but unfortunately not all audio ills.

Tips & Tricks

DeClicker is not the kind of plug-in that as soon as it you turn it on, it will turn you on. On occasion, you'll have to give it some guidance so it can zero in on sonic deadbeats. Here's how you can help it get the job done satisfactorily:

◆ Use parameter automation to dynamically control the De-Clicker parameters at troublesome spots during the treatment. This won't work with DirectX though.

◆ Make frequent use of AUDITION and listen closely if you can detect a signal that sounds like it has the same rhythm as the original. If this is the case, then DeClicker is probably misinterpreting peak pulses as clicks. To avoid the plug ›eating‹ the snap of a bass drum or the attack of a guitar pick when it processes your audio material, you should raise the THRESHOLD value.

Repeated processing of signals via the DeClicker as I recommended earlier should best be done offline. If you set up several DeClickers in series, the CPU of many a computer will toss in the towel. Besides, the influence of the parameters in the different DeClicker entities would be rather difficult to suss out.

Mastering

Many of the plug-ins discussed up to this point are of course suitable for use during mastering.

The following plug-ins are however designed exclusively for precisely this chore. Here the ability to load the plug to VST's MASTER EFFECTS rack is not just an additional option, it's actually part of the ›master‹ plan.

Prosoniq Dynasone

VST Windows	DirectX	—
	VST Pc	(in the works)
VST Macintosh		✓
Available in VST Racks		Send Effects, Channel Inserts and Master
Standard Routing		Insert or Master
World Wide Web		http://www.prosoniq.com/

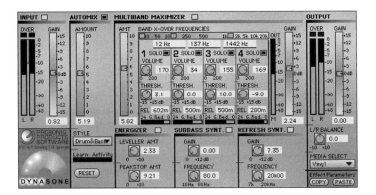

Concept

Dynasone is a combination tool that sports all the basic functions you need to make the most of a mixdown. Like the Prosoniq VoxCiter, this plug is also subdivided into separate functional blocks. Here though somebody hit the light switch—the visuals are much brighter and thus the interface of the Dynasone is considerably easier to discern. The following sections can be activated separately:

◆ INPUT: Display and control feature for the input level with an INPUT LED that serves as a front for a bypass circuit for the entire plug-in.

◆ AUTOMIX: This is something like an ›intelligent mix maximizer.‹ You can select a musical style for the mixdown from twelve choices, including ambient, pop, drum & bass. Then all you have to do is tell Dynasone to analyze the material. It figures out a suitable mix for you. You decide how much is enough of a good thing—AMOUNT lets you control the intensity of the treatment.

◆ MULTIBAND MAXIMIZER: This is a compressor that processes four frequency bands separately. You can tweak the frequency ranges of the four bands and check each band out separately via SOLO. Other band-specific parameters are Level, Compressor Threshold and Release Time. The vertically arrayed AMT fader lets you control the effects intensity of the entire section.

◆ ENERGIZER: Here you get a simple combination consisting of a wide-band compressor (LEVELLER AMT) and limiter (PEAKSTOP AMT).

◆ SUBBASS SYNT.: This is a subbass generator that allows you to add subharmonics to the bottom end and thus inject a bit more ›oomph‹ into your mix.

◆ REFRESH SYNT.: Similar stuff, but this feature does the harmonics thing with the higher frequencies, a kind of exciter you could say.

Finally, you get an OUTPUT section in which you can not only manipulate the output level, but also the stereo balance. This section is equipped with helpful level meters and/or status indicators, as are INPUT, AUTOMIX and MULTIBAND MAXIMIZER.

Next to the neutral setting, in the MEDIA SELECT menu, you can do just that with the options CD, TAPE or VINYL. The latter choice is particularly interesting because it lets you compensate for phase shifting in the bottom end. With this type of corrective action, you can end up with mixdowns that, when pressed on vinyl, have a considerably higher level—in other words, a louder record.

Inconspicuous but very important is the MEDIA SELECT menu located at the bottom edge of the window. It lets you select which medium your mix is destined for so that the plug can optimize the mix specifically for it.

Rating

Despite its many different functions, Dynasone is relatively easy to handle because each section is limited to a few key parameters. Agreeably, its appetite for CPU resources is pretty reasonable. You can also deactivate functions individually that you don't need, thus easing the load on the CPU.

The quality of the treatment varies considerably. The AUTOMIX function doesn't do it for me. For one, it's hard to discern exactly what it is that it does, for the other, when you can follow its ›reasoning,‹ you'll find that at times it's flawed. For example, if you're working with a mixdown that already has a relatively weak bottom end and activate DRUM & BASS, the bass frequencies are attenuated even more. I don't know about you, but in my book, this is not stunningly ›intelligent.‹

The Multiband Compressor on the other hand is truly a handy tool, I'd say the best the plug has to offer. Its quality is very good and, in combination with the ENERGIZER, you can pump up the loudness of the mixdown to an impressive level without having to take irritating side effects into account.

I consider SUBBASS and REFRESH SYNTH more as ›condiments,‹ terms I certainly don't use in a disparaging manner. Obviously the two sections aren't nearly as good or versatile as highly specialized plugs designed for these applications. However, if you, like many users, just want to add some high-end sparkle or punchy bottom end without a monumental effort, I'd say these will do quite nicely.

Tips & Tricks

If you never worked with a multiband compressor, it will be worth your while to take a closer look at this section of the Dynasone:

1 Activate INPUT and MULTIBAND MAXIMIZER so that you can hear what the section does without a lot of other stuff getting in the way. Be sure to deactivate AUTOMIX because otherwise you won't have manual access to the crossover frequencies of the compressor bands.

2 The three blue boxes at the upper edge of the window let you change the crossover frequencies of the four compressor bands. When you want to adjust these, be sure to audition the individual bands by activating SOLO. If at all possible, and it is admittedly a difficult task, try to set the crossover frequencies so that every crucial instrument in your mixdown is audible within one band only.

3 Remain in SOLO mode and check out the influence of THRESHOLD (the point at which the compressor kicks in) and REL (compressor release time). VOLUME has no effect here.

4 Switch SOLO off. Now you can determine the overall amount of compression (AMT) and the balance between the different frequency bands (VOLUME).

The advantage of a multiband compressor is that it generally enables you compress signals more drastically without causing the master signal to ›pump‹ audibly. Cool indeed, but there is a measure of risk involved: When you use multiband compression to process the diverse frequency bands differently, you can seriously warp the overall soundscape. Keep this in mind while you're working and use the VOLUME controls to fix the mix if you perceive a given frequency range as too dominant or weak.

You can of course exploit the over-the-top potential of this type of compressor to deliberately mess with the balance of the mix. If you manage to isolate the essential instruments in the bands, you can use the VOLUME and THRESH control to post-process the bass, guitar, snare or hi-hat individually and thus consciously tweak the balance of a given signal within the mixdown.

The MULTIBAND MAXIMIZER facilitates pretty radical manipulations. If you go overboard, the post-Maximizer ENERGIZER tends to make the mix pump—you end up with something sounding like a herd of buffalo mating. In cases like this, try out different combinations of the MULTIBAND AMT and LEVELLER AMT parameters to optimize the effect.

Waves L1

VST Windows	DirectX	✓
	VST PC	—
VST Macintosh		✓
Available in VST Racks	Send Effects, Channel Inserts and Master	
Standard Routing	Insert or Master	
World Wide Web	http://www.waves.com/	

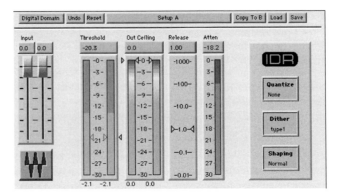

Concept

Waves L1 is what audio junkies call a ›brickwall peak lim-iter,‹ which is actually a pretty accurate description of what it does. In this type of limiter, signal peaks are flattened when they run into a given ceiling. This leaves more headroom, which is exploited by raising the overall signal to a higher level.

The plug-in comes in different versions:

◆ L1 LIMITER is a leaner version featuring some streamlined parameters; it is more suitable for processing individual rather than master signals.

- ◆ +L1 UltraMaximizer is the ›official‹ mastering plug-in featuring all the key options as well as an integrated IDR section.

In the fully loaded version, you can control the input level and stereo balance. Control freaks rejoice, ATTACK and RELEASE let you influence how quickly the limiter grabs pulse peaks and lets them go.

OUT CEILING controls the maximum level and THRESHOLD the degree to which the signal is limited.

▶ A limiter such as the L1 boosts the average level (RMS) of the signal without simultaneously increasing peak values. The signal thus has a higher average energy value—it sounds punchier and subjectively louder. This is why the technically correct term for this attribute is ›loudness.‹

Rating

I'd say the L1 is more a special application that is best used like a ›proper‹ effect—to process individual tracks. The +L1 Ultra Maximizer is another matter entirely. I would call it the *epitome* of a mastering tool.

If there is any plug that can rightfully lay claim to making everything brighter, better and more beautiful, this is it.

With its unique algorithm, the plug-in can even add impressive punch and loudness to audio material that was previously squashed by an ill-advised amount of compression. It produces just the kind of killer tone that makes pop, rock and techno tracks stand out in a crowd.

Confronted with ye olde desert island scenario and assuming I had nothing better to do in paradise than master material destined for audio CDs, vinyl or other media and productions at a professional level of quality and could have just one plug-in, it would be just me, palm trees and the +L1 Ultra-Maximizer.

▶ With a brickwall limiter like the L1, it is essential that it responds extremely quickly to incoming signal peaks. This why the L1, unlike so many of us, works along the lines of a function called ›Look Ahead:‹ the L1 gazes into a crystal ball and anticipates the digital data stream by analyzing some samples ahead of time. This allows it to limit signals extremely effectively because it isn't caught unprepared for the pulses of the input signal.

Tips & Tricks

With its integrated IDR section, the +L1 Ultra Maximizer should definitely be the final link in the digital signal processing chain when you're mastering. Use the parameter OUT CEILING to determine the ultimate threshold for the highest peaks that you want to allow in the signal because normalizing the track after the L1 has done its thing is inadvisable.

The maximum value of 100 % is hugely popular, but it's not always your best bet. If you are intending to transfer the material to U-Matic for pre-mastering, you should leave some headroom, say 0.2 dB (OUT CEILING: –0.2). Why? Because, depending on the U-Matic machine, it may shower error messages if you don't. When in doubt, ask the CD pressing people or the pre-mastering gurus which setting they recommend.

When you're mastering audio material for multimedia applications such as computer games or interactive CD-ROMs, often an even greater headroom of 2 to 3 dB is advisable because many cheap soundcards tend to produce audible distortion at a digital audio level of 100 % (0 dBFS).

Waves IDR

VST Windows	DirectX	✓
	VST PC	—
VST Macintosh		✓
Available in VST Racks		Send Effects, Channel Inserts and Master
Standard Routing		Master
World Wide Web		`http://www.waves.com/`

Concept

In case you were wondering, the abbreviation IDR stands for ›Increased Digital Resolution.‹ IDR is a technology designed to optimize audio material depending on type, technical quality and target medium. IDR ships with the Waves Native Power Pack as a separate plug in a mono and stereo version.

Yes, you do get IDR, but in a seriously stymied version. Here the only parameter you can vary is word width, which is a lot less than fully fledged IDR can give you. Incidentally, the same holds true for the IDR offshoots in +S1, +C1 or +L1.

Only the +L1 UltraMaximizer features the real IDR deal. Indeed, IDR is a key component of this bundle, because informed Waves Native Power Pack users, i.e. ones that read the previous section, always use the UltraMaximizer as the last link in the mastering chain.

The IDR section of the +L1 UltraMaximizer features just three parameters:

♦ QUANTIZE: Selects the word width of the target medium (8, 12, 16 or 20 bits).

♦ DITHER: This term pertains to a digital audio process where low-level noise is deliberately added to signal. Although it might sound a bit like dousing flames with gasoline, this noise is perceived as less annoying, so it is used to mask so-called ›quantization distortion‹.

♦ Here you can decide to pass on dithering or chose one of the following two options:

TYPE 1, recommended for 16- or 20-bit mastering, and

TYPE 2, less aggressive than TYPE 1, thus less noise, but more quantization distortion; recommended for 8- or 12-bit mastering.

♦ SHAPING: Noise shaping shifts the added energy inherent in the noise to a higher frequency range, which makes it more difficult for our ears to hear. Here this range is above 15 kHz. Aside from passing on noise shaping entirely, you can select either MODERATE for 8- or 12-bit mastering, NORMAL and ULTRA.

Rating

If you're reluctant to make a decision whether or not to buy an IDR plug-in, don't. This technology only comes as an add-on feature of other plug-ins. IDR is recommended whenever you want to squeeze a digital production into as small a word width as possible with as little signal loss as possible. This is for instance the case when you want to convert a 16-bit recording to 12 bits for a multimedia application.

For the 16-bit CD audio format, IDR is good to have when quantization distortion starts giving you headaches. This generally happens when you're working with material featuring extreme dynamics, say a brief passage that sounds like a Chinese New Year's celebration, immediately followed by something hushed like the sound of a mite coughing, and want it to come across clear, undistorted and free of noise. Yes, this is an over-the-top analogy, but you catch my drift.

MIDI dance or techno productions are less susceptible to this kind of problem; in acoustic recordings—say of a jazz trio, classical guitar or string quartet—it tends to crop up quite frequently. If you use IDR judiciously for this kind of stuff, you will definitely end up with considerably enhanced signal quality.

Practical Tips

IDR affects primarily low signal levels and is thus not easy to suss when you're monitoring tracks at volumes that won't make your neighbors loath you with a passion.

When you're trying to figure out which DITHER parameter is most effective, try setting the quantization to 8 bits because this generates the highest level of distortion, which of course means the masking effect is most audible. If you're really planning on going for the 8-bit output format, use dithering for 44.1-kHz files only. For all other sampling rates, make sure you deactivate it.

When you're auditioning for a suitable noise shaping setting, be sure to also switch dithering off. This is the only way you will hear how the original signal is affected when its energy is shifted.

▶ You may have guessed that ULTRA is the extreme SHAPING algorithm for 16- or 20-bit mastering. It will deliver the best audio results, but because of the relatively large amount of energy that is shifted to the upper frequency range, theoretically there is the danger of undesirable side effects such as clicks when the track is played back on inferior CD or DAT players. Use this mode only when you are absolutely certain that this is the final processing stage.

Analyzers

No one would complain about a lack of level indicators in VST, these displays are all over the place. But how about viewing the energy content of the different frequencies and seeing how it is distributed throughout the mix? What about stereo displays and mono compatibility? If you want to find out what's really going inside a signal, you'll have to send it to the shrink.

To see all this stuff and more, you'll need an analyzer. Like a real psychiatrist, this kind of plug-in put's a dent in your allowance and just sits there mute as an effigy. It doesn't do a thing as far making neat noises goes, which is why most potential users would rather invest in something that does. This would be unwise. An analyzer is a boon to both pros and newbies—a standard tool for the former, an invaluable learning aid for the latter.

▶ Don't confuse the functionality of an analyzer with the analysis algorithms found in audio editing programs. The latter generally work offline only and then display average values exclusively. An analyzer works in realtime—its display hops up and down like a herd of amphetamine-crazed kangaroos. Seriously though, only a ›live‹ indicator will let you view what is happening throughout your mixdown.

Waves PAZ

VST Windows	DirectX	—
	VST PC	—
VST Macintosh		✓
Available in VST Racks		Send Effects, Channel Inserts and Master
Standard Routing		Insert or Master
World Wide Web		http://www.waves.com/

Concept

PAZ (›**P**sychoacoustic **A**naly**Z**er‹) consolidates all crucial analyzer functions on a single interface. Here you get three clearly differentiated display areas:

◆ FREQUENCY: In the large field at the top of the window, you'll see how energy is distributed among the different frequency ranges. Set to its most coarse resolution, the display comprises a range of 4 Hz to 20 kHz horizontally and is scaled logarithmically. Levels are displayed vertically within a range of –80 to 0 dB. The arrow symbols next to the display let you zoom in different directions.

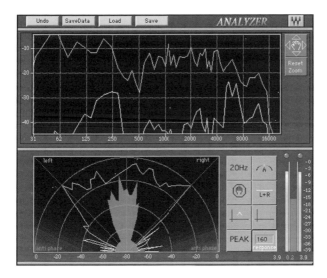

◆ POSITION: The stereo position, also referred to as the degree of correlation, is shown in the display at the bottom left field. A ›healthy‹ stereo mixdown appears in the form of a cloud. Any deviations from this ideal shape tells you that something is amiss with the stereo spread of the signal.

The widely recognized weighted modes A, B and C deal with output levels as they are perceived by the human ear. This means that the frequency ranges which the human ear is more sensitive to are weighted. Mode A is designed for low, Mode B for middle and Mode C for high monitoring or playback levels. Usually Mode A is measured, which at lower levels elicits lower results than with Mode B or C.

◆ METER: At the bottom right, you'll find two bar displays for the level of the left and right stereo channels. A wider level meter is sandwiched between the two, it represents the master signal of both channels. Only this center meter responds to the different display options. Additional numeric headroom display indicators are located at the bottom; you can reset these separately by clicking on them.

The big buttons at the bottom right let you select diverse options that influence the characteristics of the different displays. Here are the most important ones:

◆ Hz: This determines the raster for frequency analysis below 250 Hz. The standard position with the finest resolution is 40 Hz. The settings 20 or even 10 Hz have the advantage that the rest of the frequency range is displayed in greater detail.

◆ WEIGHT: Next to an unweighted display of level and frequency response, you can choose from the standard weighted modes A, B and C.

◆ SHOW: Here you can view additional curves showing peak values. This is something like a ›memory function‹ which you can of course reset to a neutral value at any time.

◆ PEAK/RMS: Use this feature to chose if you want the plug to analyze the peak or the more sluggish RMS (›summed average‹) characteristics of the signal.

◆ RESPONSE: For the record, this determines how fast the display reacts.

Rating

Waves, noted for its prolific plug policy, wouldn't be Waves if after installing the PAZ it hadn't suddenly multiplied like a couple of bored jack rabbits. You'll find each section of the plug-in also comes as a dedicated plug, which extends your plug-in selection list by six entries.

To be honest, I don't find this particularly sensible: Considering that this realtime analyzer knocks out a bunch of functions that require mondo computing, the PAZ goes amazingly easy on CPU resources. Then of course there's the fact that the CPU load of the different versions doesn't vary by anything worth mentioning, all of which leads me to raise the question of purpose.

Other than this, the only other cause for complaint is that you can't ›freeze‹ the depicted curves and save them for future reference. If in the hopes of doing just that you press the SAVE DATA button, you'll be bitterly disappointed that the only things the plug saves are the numeric values of the individual frequency bands in the form of a text table.

Everything else about PAZ is praiseworthy: the plug-in is a to date unique combination of all key audio analyzer displays.

Its versatile display options round out the hip features of this plug. All displays respond quickly enough when the plug runs on standard computers. The entire concept of this program is very practical and close to its real-world counterpart. Individual frequencies can be localized quickly and precisely.

Currently, PAZ is unfortunately only available for the Macintosh. If you are primarily interested in a spectrum analyzer, Steinberg/Spectral Design Free Filter is a good alternative for both Macintosh and PC (see page 103).

Tips & Tricks

For most users, POSITION is probably the least familiar of the three PAZ displays. Here are few tips on interpreting its information:

- The extreme stereo positions ›mono left‹ and ›mono right‹ are indicated via diagonal, unfortunately nearly impossible to discern LEFT/RIGHT lines. In other words, whenever the display depicts data as a line, you know you're dealing with purely a mono signal. If this line coincides say with the LEFT line, then the mono signal was positioned hard right in the mix.

- Normally, and in most cases ideally, the stereo mixdown appears in the shape of something close enough to a mushroom cloud that this is what I'll use to describe it. This mushroom cloud lies between the LEFT/RIGHT lines: the wider the cloud, the more stereo spread in the signal.

◆ If the cloud is relatively narrow, then too many signals in the mix are placed in the center of the stereo image. Use the PAN faders for some of the VST audio channels to spread them out a bit.

◆ If the cloud has a hole or dent at its center, you are looking at the opposite extreme. In this case, use the PAN faders to move some of the signals in the mix closer to the center of the soundscape.

◆ If at the bottom of the display it shows signals in the red ANTI-PHASE area, this indicates that portions of this signal are anti-phase. These will cancel each other out when you monitor the mix in mono, which of course can have a drastic effect on the balance of the mix.

When you run into this kind of situation, use SOLO for the individual VST audio tracks to hear which signals are causing the problems. Often the error sources are stereo tracks where you accidentally inverted the polarity. The internal VST plug-in Stereo Wizard can in some cases fix this kind of problem.

Now we'll heap some attention on the up to this point terribly neglected FREQUENCY display. Here are some pointers that will help you quickly get the hang of this tool:

1 Click on the FREQUENCY display. A freely movable set of crosshairs will appear. Place them at the point of intersection, it displays the level and frequency in numeric values. This option lets you do stuff like read the values for a peak pulse that you consider too high so that you'll know which frequency needs to be EQed.

2 Click on the FREQUENCY display while holding the ⟨alt⟩ key down. This freezes the current status of the display until you release the mouse button. Incidentally, this operation works in all other displays as well.

3 Hold the ⟨alt⟩ key down and drag the mouse to draw a box in the FREQUENCY display. This automatically defines a zoom segment.

4 Grab the hand icon next to the display and drag it via the mouse. This lets you conveniently move the visible segment of the frequency response graphic.

5 A ⌘-click on the display restores the smallest possible zoom status.

▶ PAZ offers a load of options for evaluation curves, resolution, response time and much more. Nevertheless, you don't have to be a professionally trained audio engineer to use the plug-in gainfully.

Define a standard setting and save it as a PRESET. Import some of your favorite mixdowns from CD into VST and take a good long look at these in PAZ. Compare these audio EKGs to your mixdowns and you will be able to draw a comparison between what you and your studio heroes were up to and tweak your mixes accordingly.

Packs and Bundles

Although along with assorted livestock and possibly the odd human these may have been what you had to climb over when boarding the bus on your last trip through South America, in the digital audio world these terms mean something else entirely. These are what the plug-in makers' marketing masterminds call product packages consisting of several individual plug-ins. This is often akin to the ›family size‹ mega-boxed found in supermarkets: you buy more of what the manufacturer has to offer in terms of plug-ins and get a discount for shopping in bulk.

Often you have no choice but to go for the jumbo package if you have a hankering for a given plug-in. Marketing minds work in mysterious ways, which is why some plugs aren't available on their own.

Arboretum Hyperprism

VST Windows	DirectX	✓
	VST Pc	—
VST Macintosh		✓
Available in VST Racks	Send Effects, Channel Inserts and Master	
Standard Routing	Send or Insert	
World Wide Web	http://www.arboretum.com/	

Concept

Hyperprism is a bundle consisting of many relatively simple plug-ins, most of which come in a DirectX as well as a VST Macintosh version. If you wanted to put forth the effort, and I did, you could class these in the following categories:

◆ REVERB: room reverb, regular reverb
◆ DELAY: single delay, multi delay, echo
◆ FILTERS: low pass filter, high pass filter, band pass filter, band reject filter

◆ SOUND DESIGN: ring modulator, 26-band vocoder, pitch changer, sonic decimator

◆ MODULATION: phaser, flanger, chorus, tremolo, vibrato

◆ DYNAMICS: noise gate, compressor, stereo dynamics

◆ STEREO: quasi stereo, more stereo, pan, auto pan, m-s matrix

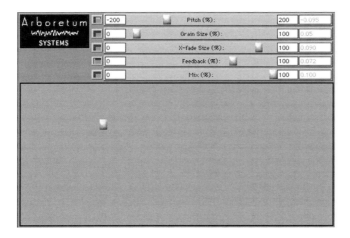

Here's stuff you'll find in the DirectX package only:

◆ Frequency Shifter—a frequency shifter modulated by an LFO for sound design

◆ HyperVerb—a new reverb algorithm

◆ Limiter—a brickwall limiter

To make amends for this blatant favoritism, Macintosh VST users also get a couple exclusive treats:

◆ EchoTranz (pitch shift effects via delay time modulation) and

◆ Doppler (Doppler effect, pitch transposition).

All Hyperprism plug-ins make do with a few essential parameters and feature a uniform user interface. All parameters are controlled via separate faders located at the top section of the control panel.

The so-called Blue Window is a special feature. Here you get a blue-colored corral with a little handle all by its lonesome. You can drag it all over the Blue Window via mouse and thus ›wrangle‹ (remote control) a herd of parameters simultaneously, kind of like a joystick.

Which parameters are influenced by which direction of movement is determined by clicking on the little blue boxes to the left of the parameter faders. If you activate a horizontal bar, then the corresponding parameter is manipulated by moving the handle horizontally. If you chose a vertical bar for a parameter—you guessed it—moving the handle vertically influences the parameter.

The truly captivating aspect of this feature is that with just a few mouse clicks, you can conjure up more complex assignments for the Blue Window. Then, completely unaware and unconcerned of what the outcome will be, you can fumble with the handle at random to generate surprising results.

Rating

You shouldn't consider Hyperprism a universal plug-in package that will spare you the investment in a reverb, delay, compressor and the like. Most of the effects here sound pretty much standard, the attraction of the bundle lies elsewhere—the Blue Window to be precise. The dynamic parameter roller-coaster rides that it enables will let you come up with spectacular sound manipulations.

Not all components of the bundle benefit by an equal measure from the Blue Window remote control. Standard effects such as reverb, delay or the limiter are not particularly well suited to this type of manipulation. Where you will get a thrill is when you use it in conjunction with sound design and modulation effects. The pitch and frequency shift algorithms in particular are mind-blowing. You'll undoubtedly be impressed by how quickly and at the same time smoothly Hyperprism executes even the wildest parameter rides. This little gizmo lets you come up with stuff like tape-stop effects—i.e. throttling the pitch and tempo in a split-second—in an incomparable level of quality.

On the downside, both VST compatible Hyperprism packages are marred by some pretty glaring flaws:

♦ DIRECTX: With something like the BLUE WINDOW at your disposal, you would think that like no other plug-in, the Hyperprism begs to have its parameter rides recorded via VST automation. In the VST Macintosh version this is entirely possible, which may just be the most compelling reason to buy Hyperprism. Pretty much everyone in the business knows that automation won't ›fly‹ in DirectX, so why Arboretum decided to of all options release this bundle for the Windows platform as a DirectX version will remain a mystery known only to the company's strategists.

♦ VST Macintosh: Of all the plugs I have figuratively held in my hot little hands—and believe, there have been a bunch—Hyperprism is among the most unstable. Dismayingly, crashes are customary.

For these reasons, I can't recommend Hyperprism to VST users without some reservations. Then why did I bother figuratively bending your ear about it? Because its concept as well as some of the algorithms are totally unique, incomparable to anything I've come across.

If in reading about them you developed an urge to try these effects on for size, there's only one way to go—Hyperprism. You'll just have to learn to live with its disadvantages.

If you're a model of patience, I'd say keep on eye on how this bundle evolves and hope that its imperfections are squared away in time.

Tips & Tricks

If you activate BLUE WINDOW control for all parameters, it looks pretty wild, but you'll find it impossible to handle with any degree of accuracy. You'll coax the most convincing effects out of Hyperprism when you limit the fun and games to one parameter each for the X and Y axis.

On the left and right side of each parameter fader in the Hyperprism plug-ins, you'll find white boxes that display numeric values. These indicate the value range of the individual fader.

When you have some time on your hands, try moving each fader to see which parameter values deliver the most interesting sounds. Often it's just a tiny segment of the available value range that will give you anything worthwhile. Once you have identified what works for you, click on the white boxes and enter smaller peak and bottom values for the parameters via keyboard or mouse to narrow down their ranges.

Now the faders work in a more ›sensible‹ value range and you can tweak the parameters more subtly. This measure is particularly appropriate for the BLUE WINDOW.

Waves Native Power Pack (NPP)

VST Windows	DirectX	✓
	VST PC	—
VST Macintosh	✓	
Available in VST Racks	Send Effects, Channel Inserts and Master	
Standard Routing	Send or Insert	
World Wide Web	http://www.waves.com/	

This is presumably *the* Standard plug-in package, it has been out on the market forever and thus enjoys widespread use. The following plug-ins, all of which were discussed in detail earlier—are part of the bundle:

- ◆ TrueVerb reverb (see page 74)
- ◆ Q10 Parametric EQ (see page 98)
- ◆ C1 Compressor/Gate/Expander (see page 135)
- ◆ S1 Stereo Imager (see page 176)
- ◆ L1 Limiter/Ultra-Maximizer (see page 190)

◆ IDR Dithering (see page 192)

▶ All of these plug-ins cannot be purchased individually, you have to buy the entire Native Power Pack.

You also get the ›Track Pac lite‹ software, which is designed to do something called ›file compression.‹ This has nothing to do with an audio compressor. Here audio files are packed via a special algorithm sans signal degradation so that they take up less space when you archive them on a storage medium.

In this pack you also get WaveKey, a hardware copy protection key that you have to insert into your computer—the ADB port of the Macintosh, the LPT printer interface on a PC. This enterprising system lets you buy other Waves plug-ins online. If you fork over cash up front, you get a serial number that works only in combination with your unique WaveKey and enables the plug-in on your computer. If you want to buy another Waves plug-in such as the Renaissance Compressor, De-Esser or MaxxBass and do not own the NPP, you'll have to buy the WavesKey separately.

Although all plugs of the NPP are worth the money, in my opinion its flagships are the TrueVerb and L1. You'll have to figure out for yourself if the NPP is a reasonable investment for you, although it should help you make an informed decision if you read the individual sections on each plug.

The advantages of this pack certainly include its comprehensive range of plug-ins—you get all the basic effects and processors—and its good audio quality. Not everyone will be thrilled by its user interfaces—many of them have a highly technical look and feel and some of the functions require an uncommonly keen ability to think abstractly, which is nothing more than windy way of saying they're hard to figure out.

The CPU appetite of some of the plugs is Marlon Brando-esque, which means you'll need a beefy computer indeed.

For the Macintosh platform, Waves offers the Gold Bundle. The company should win the ›Truth in Marketing‹ award for the bundle's name even if the gold standard is defunct: as it was originally designed for the TDM platform, you'll have to fork over lots of pennies for it. The good news is that you get every Waves plug-in under the sun; the bad, since you get all native versions in this bundle, the Gold package is not all that desirable for VST users.

Tc Works Native Bundle

Vst Windows	DirectX	✓
	Vst Pc	✓
Vst Macintosh	✓	
Available in Vst Racks	Send Effects, Channel Inserts and Master	
Standard Routing	Send, Insert and Master	
World Wide Web	`http://www.tcworks.com/`	

Brand spanking new and available at a moderate price is the Native Bundle by Tc Works. With it, you get the following plug-ins:

◆ Native Reverb (see page 79)

◆ Native Eq filter package (see page 94)

◆ Native DeX Compressor/De-Esser (see page 215)

In due time, this bundle will undoubtedly give the Waves Npp stiff competition. Yes, neither the range nor the complexity of effects is up to snuff with the Waves Npp, but many a user will welcome its less-is-more concept.

The Tc algorithms all sound good, the user interfaces are very easy to fathom and they offer a host of imaginative details. The plugs' Cpu requirements are all relatively moderate. If you pitted the two reverbs—Waves TrueVerb and Tc Works Native Reverb—against each other in a head-to-head shootout, this would be one of the first things you'd notice.

There is another advantage the Tc bundle has over the Waves Npp on the Windows Pc platform: Here the majority of the plugs come not only in a DirectX, but also a Vst Pc version. You can thus automate the die Tc plug-ins in Vst Windows, whereas, read and weep, this is a no-go with the Npp plug-ins.

To make a long story shorter, if you like the sonic equivalent of novelle cuisine—lots of frills and exotic tweaking options—then Npp is the pack for you. If instead you're a meat-

and-potatoes girl or guy, like stuff simple, straight-forward and can do without some of the more inventive parameters, then the Tc Native Bundle is a great alternative.

Tc Works Native Essentials

VST Windows	DirectX	✓
	VST Pc	—
VST Macintosh	—	
Available in VST Racks	Send Effects, Channel Inserts and Master	
Standard Routing	Send, Insert and Master	
World Wide Web	http://www.tcworks.com/	

This is a set of three simple plug-ins, each of which is definitely a ›budget‹ version of a more luxuriously appointed Tc Native plug. The user interfaces are uniform: At the left, you'll always find a display for the input level and a corresponding control. The rest of the control features are limited to the bare, hence the name, essentials:

◆ Q is a simple parametric EQ comparable to the Native EQ-P (see page 94). The junior plug-in makes do with three frequency bands. Although you don't get a frequency response display here, everything else is identical to the bands on the plug's big brother—fully parametric with four variable filter characteristics each.

The joystick at the right is kind of cute. You can switch it to each of the three bands by turns to fiddle with cutoff frequency and gain simultaneously.

◆ R is the poor (wo)man's Tc Native Reverb (see page 79). Your twiddling options are limited to the ›Lc Display‹ of the Native Reverb. In other words, all you can do is call up one of the presets and goof around with the decay and effects balance.

◆ X is a basic compressor, you could call it a runt Native DeX (see page 215). Not bad considering you can not only influence THRESHOLD and RATIO, but also vary its response via ATTACK and RELEASE. Finally, you get a dynamic RE-DUCTION display that indicates the measure by which levels are being attenuated, a switchable SOFT SAT function designed to combat digital distortion and a SOFT KNEE option for particularly smooth compression curves.

This bundle is in many respects the logical distillation of the Tc Native bundle: fewer functions, more compact, easier to handle. If the Tc Native were a Hollywood production, the Essentials would a low-budget indie prequel. However, these functions are enough to float many a boat. If yours is among them—at least for the time being—then I can do no other than recommend this package highly. The effects sound very good and its Cpu load is laughably low: this is the ideal bundle for newbies.

► With EasyWaves, Waves released a similar ›utility grade‹ package. Although the other Waves plug-ins are all fine, regrettably I can't say the same for EasyWaves. Its effects are not just bare-bones simple, they also sound it. If you're in the market for this type of package, the Tc Native Essentials is the better choice by far. Too bad that they're available for the Windows Pc platform only.

Object Productions Vintage Fx Bundle

Vst Windows	DirectX	(in the works)
	Vst Pc	✓
Vst Macintosh	✓	
Available in Vst Racks	Send Effects, Channel Inserts and Master	
Standard Routing	Send, Insert and Master	
World Wide Web	`http://www.vintagefx.com/`	

With the Vintage Fx Bundle, Object Productions a.k.a. Jordan Bortz offers an inexpensive plug-in package for both Vst computer platforms. It contains all of the plugs featured in the two earlier Object Productions packages Vintage Power Pak. Vol 1 and Power Insert Pak. This is a comprehensive processor set including reverb, stereo compressor, limiter, different Eqs featuring three to seven bands, delays and modulation effects.

The quality of these effects varies considerably: The reverb won't gladden anybody's heart no matter how undemanding. The Vst-internal plugs or a freeware plug-in such as xVerb will serve you better. The delays and Eqs are okay but won't make you think you're hearing the plug package scream ›Buy me‹ when you're checking it out.

However, the diverse modulation effects such as the Chorus, Flanger, Nu-Tron Phaser, Multi-Fx and Band Chorus will.

These also emulate the VST standard rack interface and thus don't look like ›boutique‹ effects, but their sound smokes. The phased and chorused sounds are among the best yours truly has ever heard from VST-compatible plugs.

If you're on a quest for convincing, very ›analog‹ sounding modulation effects, you should definitely lend the demo plug-ins of this pack your ear.

5 Kiss the Future

Or maybe an awkward hug will do too. Anyway, you may have noticed that new generations of plug-ins seem to be debuting at increasingly shorter intervals, so I thought you might appreciate a brief glimpse into the crystal ball. In this chapter, we'll look at four interesting plug-ins which hadn't been released at the time this book went to press, which of course means I couldn't scope out a release version. By the time you are thumbing through these pages, these promising newcomers should already be available.

All of the information in this chapter was provided by the manufacturers. However, most plug-ins were almost ready for release when my editor coerced me into to handing over the manuscript for this book, so there shouldn't have been any radical changes.

Apogee MasterTools

VST Windows	DirectX	—
	VST PC	✓
VST Macintosh		✓
Standard Routing	Master or Insert	
World Wide Web	`http://www.apogee.com/`	

This plug-in features a combination of a dithering algorithm and spectrum display. Since Waves IDR is kind of like the frosting on the Waves NPP cake, or more accurately its plugs, you wouldn't be amiss in calling the MasterTools the only stand-alone dithering tool for VST. The plug-in was designed in a collaborative effort by Steinberg/Spectral Design and Apogee. MasterTools features three fundamental signal processing functions:

♦ DITHERING: Word widths of up to 24 bits can be converted to the current standard for the CD audio format, 16-bit word width.

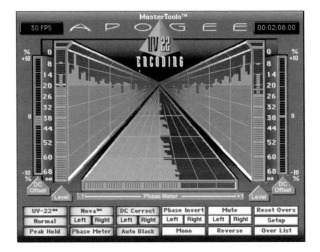

◆ METER: Here you get a total of eight different display options for viewing different aspects of signals such as level or phase position. Of particular interest is the 3-D display equipped with a five-second buffer. Here you can view a display reaction long after it would have disappeared into oblivion on conventional display instruments.

◆ CORRECTION: Finally, with this feature you can manipulate certain aspects of a signal directly. For example, you can swap the two stereo channels, change the phase length or eliminate D.C. (DC CORRECT) in signals.

You could consider the latter two a capable supporting cast, but the dithering function is without a doubt the real star of the show. Here Apogee employed the legendary UV-22 algorithm. This dithering mechanism is normally reserved for ultra-expensive hardware products such as high-end sample rate converters or the Mackie Design digital console d8b.

If you want to put together a high-end system with 24-bit AD converters for VST and need 16-bit conversion that ensures minimum signal degradation for CD audio productions, then Apogee MasterTools will probably be your first choice.

Tc Works Native DeX

Vsᴛ Windows	DirectX	✓
	Vsᴛ Pc	✓
Vsᴛ Macintosh	—	
Standard Routing	Insert-effect	
World Wide Web	http://www.tcworks.com/	

Tc Native DeX is a compressor/de-esser, the concept and user interface of which are reminiscent of the other Tc Native series plug-ins, and unsurprisingly is also available as part of the Tc Native bundles. The two processing functions can be used separately or in tandem if you prefer:

♦ Compressor: Here you can vary the standard parameters:
  Attack—response time of 0.1 to 50 ms,
  Release—response time of 20 to 2,000 ms,
  Threshold—level ceiling,
  Ratio—degree of compressions from 1.0:1 to 64:1 and
  Hold Time.

You also get a button that lets you set the compressor to SOFT KNEE mode, i. e. make it work with a flatter compression curve for especially inconspicuous processing. The compression curve can also be shaped via the SOFT KNEE fader.

♦ DE-ESSER: This section is pre-compressor in the plug's signal chain, but it can be switched off whenever desired. Here you can define the cutoff frequency and the degree of attenuation. You can listen to the De-esser's control signal in isolation (MONITOR).

Like the Waves C1, this plug-in ships with a sidechain function for the compressor. The sidechain in the DeX however is hipper by virtue of greater versatility:

The sidechain signal is routed to DeX in a similar manner as in the Prosoniq Orange Vocoder. This is presumably the best and most flexible option for processing the audio signals of different VST audio channels collectively in a plug-in.

It features its very own KEY INPUT plug-in, which you can plug into another VST audio channel as an Insert ›effect.‹ Its sole purpose is to tap into the signal and pipe it to the compressor section of the DeX.

You can use up to two KEY INPUT plug-ins in other channels and then in DeX determine which of the two control signals will influence the section (KEY INPUT 1/2). This means that you can reroute any audio signal from the VST mixer and use it as a sidechain feed for the DeX.

This plug-in—like the other Tc Native plugs—features the SOFT SAT algorithm, which helps combat digital distortion. Next to displays for in- and output levels, the DeX is equipped with dynamic displays for compression ratio and level of the KEY signal.

The Native DeX also comes with a little circuit called AUTO MAKEUP GAIN. It automatically sets the plug-in's output to 0 dB at all times. This is pretty handy because after you've changed a compressor parameter, you don't have to twiddle the output level knob manually to compensate for the level you altered internally.

Native DeX comprises all important aspects of dynamics processing in a clear, concise plug-in. The finer points of this plug include the option of combining compressor and de-esser functions freely as well as the variable sidechain concept. If its sound quality ends up comparable to that of the other Tc Native plug-ins, the upstart Native DeX will present some serious competition to its entrenched Waves rivals.

Steinberg/Spectral Design Multicomp

VST Windows	DirectX	✓
	VST Pc	✓
VST Macintosh		✓
Available in VST Racks	Send Effects, Channel Inserts and Master	
Standard Routing	Insert or Master	
World Wide Web	`http://spectral-design.com/`	

This is a multiband compressor that works along much the same lines as the compressor section of the Prosoniq Dynasone (see page 186). Multicomp however operates with five frequency bands, for each of which you can determine the compression curve individually.

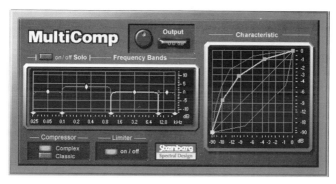

Next to the ›classic‹ compressor algorithm, the plug features the imaginatively named NEW mode designed to prevent the typical pumping phenomenon via an ›intelligent‹ control circuit. You also a get a completely independent LIMITER which you can activate along with the compression, which is recommended when you're using the Multicomp for mastering.

Two displays give you visual references: FREQUENCY BANDS defines the distribution of the five frequency bands, CHARACTERISTIC controls the compressor curve. Each band can of course be auditioned separately, which is something you can hardly do without on a multiband compressor.

Although Multicomp and Waves L1 take a different approach, the issue that will decide if the new Steinberg/Spectral Design plug is a winner or a dud is if it's in the same league as the classic Waves plug in terms of delivering killer compression and maximum loudness.

Steinberg/Spectral Design Quadrafuzz

VST Windows	DirectX	✓
	VST Pc	✓
VST Macintosh		✓
Available in VST Racks	Send Effects, Channel Inserts and Master	
Standard Routing	Insert or Master	
World Wide Web	http://spectral-design.com/	

This plug is based on a circuit developed by my esteemed American colleague, Craig Anderton—contributor to Electronic Musician, Guitar Player and Keyboard among others—many years ago. Much the same as in Multicomp, here the signal is split into several frequency bands, four to be exact. You are of course free to define the crossover frequencies.

Although the individual frequency bands are not compressed individually, they are distorted individually, which in my book is a heck of a lot more fun.

The world of sound-chiseling options that this feature opens up is beyond anything that a normal distortion plug-in can do. Not only can you use the Quadrafuzz to add grit to guitar and bass signals, it is also great for making vocals, keyboards and drum loops sound bigger, better and more lively.

6 The Hippest Freeware Plug-ins

Today there are oodles of plug-ins out there that you can own without spending whatever is the smallest denomination of your currency, which presumably is why they are called freeware plug-ins.

Of course many of these suffer from the ›I-can't-do-it-any-better-than-the-pros-but-at-least-it's-got-my-name-on-it‹ syndrome. However, there are some freeware plug-ins that can go toe-to-toe with their commercial ›rivals‹ and at the minimum, battle them to a draw.

Since you can download freeware plug-ins from the Internet (see page 240 for Www addresses) and will also find the majority of exponents of this breed of plug on the included CD-Rom, you can try these programs to no end, or at least until your spouse threatens divorce.

For precisely these reasons—because you can see for yourself and I don't want to sabotage your relationship—I've kept this chapter on freeware plug-ins short and sweet. The latter is the point really, to whet your appetite for more.

In addition to the freeware plug-ins mentioned here, there are many more that may not deliver quite the spectacular bang, but can in many situations be just the right tool to get the job done. This is why—time allowing—you should check out all the other freeware plug-ins on the included CD-Rom!

Aldo Trianti—xVerb

VST Windows	DirectX	—
	VST Pc	✓
VST Macintosh		—
Available in VST Racks	Send Effects, Channel Inserts and Master	
Standard Routing	Send (Post-fader)	
World Wide Web	`http://members.xoom.com/atrianti/` `start.htm`	

Most of the more unusual freeware plug-ins attract attention because they are based on an exotic concept or feature a bizarre interface. Neither applies to the xVerb plug-in by the Italian programmer Aldo Trianti, but it does deliver a universally desired standard effect in a very good quality—reverb.

xVerb is a plug-in designed for standard Vst racks. Here's a survey of some of its editable parameters:

Size—room acerage,
Decay—post reverb fade out,
Damp—high frequency damping,
Early—balance between early reflections and reverb tail,
Density—›thickness‹ of the reverb tail and
Mix—mono- or stereo-compatible output signal.

The xVerb demands several times the Cpu resources of the WunderVerb3, even considerably more than the ESpacial. On the sunny side, xVerb sounds substantially better than the internal Vst reverb plug-ins—especially when you dial in softer reverb tails for mid-sized rooms.

The only drawback of xVerb is only a drawback if you happen to be a Macintosh user, but then its the ultimate downer: currently it comes in a Vst Pc version only.

If you own a semi-tough Windows Pc and don't feel like investing you're hard-earned in an expensive commercial reverb plug-in such as Waves TrueVerb, definitely install xVerb!

Dave Brown—Tempo Delay

VST Windows	DirectX	✓
	VST Pc	✓
VST Macintosh	✓	
Available in VST Racks	Send Effects, Channel Inserts and Master	
Standard Routing	Send (Post-fader)	
World Wide Web	http://www.dbrown.force9.co.uk/	

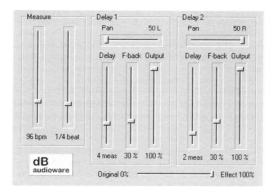

The English programmer Dave Brown didn't think much of the internal VST Stereo Echo, so, obviously an industrious individual, he decided to write a few alternatives with the help of the Steinberg VST Software Development Kit.

One of the programs he came up with is the Tempo Delay. Alongside the VST Pc and VST Macintosh versions featuring the a standard rack interface, there is now a DirectX version with its own graphical interface.

The features of the Tempo Delay are largely identical to those of the internal VST plug-in Stereo Echo. Here too, you get two separate delay chains with individually variable feedback, panorama and level. The cool thing about Tempo Delay is that you don't have to mess around with a calculator or have a conversion chart handy while you're working because it indicates the delay rates in musical values rather than millisecond intervals:

TEMPO lets you define—who would have guessed—the song tempo (30 to 250 BPM), BEAT the note value ($^1/_{16}$ and $^1/_1$), and MEASURES (1 to 32) the number of bars.

Here's how you enter a musically appropriate delay value:

1   Set TEMPO to the given song tempo. If the song's tempo is not a whole number, i.e. it lies somewhere between two values, set the next higher or lower value by ear. Most of the time, this minute a difference won't be audible.

2   If your song is in $^4/_4$ time, start with a MEASURE value of 4. This is in any case the default.

3   The BEAT parameter delivers what the parameter values promises: $^1/_{16}$ produces a $^1/_{16}$ delay, $^1/_8$ a $^1/_8$ delay. Values of three will give you ternary rhythms.

4   If the feel is right and you want to simply halve or double a delay time, use the MEASURE parameter for this purpose. For example, if you want to turn a $^1/_4$ delay into a $^1/_8$ delay, halve the MEASURE value—in this particular example, you would of course enter 2 for the MEASURE parameter.

5   Here's a nifty bit of delay groove trickery: For binary rhythms such as $^4/_4$, be sure to try ternary delays (BEAT $^1/_3$, $^1/_6$ etc.). Often this will produce a complex syncopated and usually substantially more interesting overall groove.

Musically ›meaningful‹ echoes or taps if you prefer are easy as pie to implement in Tempo Delay. The delays are substantially longer than in VST's own Stereo Echo, yet the sound quality is identical. The Tempo Delay's CPU requirements are roughly equivalent to those of the Stereo Echo.

All in all, the Tempo Delay beats the internal VST Stereo Echo plug-in hands down. I have but one thing to say to every VST Windows user who does not install this freeware plug-in—hope you're feeling better soon, if not get professional help.

▶ For the VST PC interface, Dave Brown also came up with the freeware plug-in Sweep Delay. Although you get just one delay chain, you can have the effects signal sweep through the panorama continuously, kind of like an integrated auto-panner. To manipulate the panorama modulation, you can tweak the parameters PAN (panorama output value), MOD SPEED (modulation rate from 0.1 to 20 Hz) and MOD WIDTH (modulation width from 0 to 100%).

The maximum delay time at 44.1 kHz is four seconds, which is twice as long as that of the Tempo Delay. This means that Sweep Delay is a good alternative for ultra-long Fx taps.

Vellocet VReOrder

VST Windows	DirectX	—
	VST PC	✓
VST Macintosh	✓	
Available in VST Racks	Send Effects and Channel Inserts	
Standard Routing	Send (Pre-fader) or Insert	
World Wide Web	http://vellocet.ii.net/	

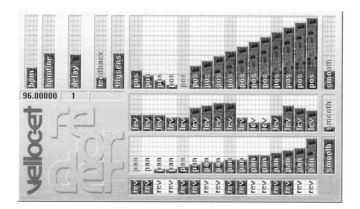

The Australian musicians and programmers SKoT McDonald and Andrew Simper have come up with several good freeware plug-ins, but VReOrder definitely takes the cake.

This unusual plug-in is somewhat of a challenge to de-scribe, ›sampler/audio shredder/manipulator‹ might come close. What it really does is hard to put your finger on, but its decidedly worth investigating. Here the learn-by-doing method seems appropriate:

1 Position a single-bar mono drum loop (as simple as possible, $\frac{4}{4}$ time) in VST ARRANGE. Load VReOrder to the SEND EFFECTS rack and patch the signal to it from the given VST MIXER channel as a PRE-fader effect. For this purpose, turn EFFECT SEND up, switch the PRE button on and pull the channel fader all the way down.

2 In ARRANGE, set the L Locator to a position equivalent to one bar prior to the start of the loop, the R Locator to two bars following the end of the loop. Make sure that these intervals are truly blank so that you won't hear anything else when you play the effect back.

3 Call up the EDIT window of VReOrder but definitely do not change any of the settings!

4 Set the tempo of your loop at the left. Accuracy is essential here, which is why the plug features coarse and fine tuning parameters for BPM.

5 With the DELAY parameter, you can determine the length of the sam-ple that VReOrder takes from the incoming audio material. You have a range of $\frac{1}{32}$ to two $\frac{1}{1}$ notes to choose from. For the time being, select ›1,‹ which in $\frac{4}{4}$ time is equivalent to the length of one bar.

6 TRIGSENS lets you vary the signal level at which VReOrder start ›record-ing‹ the plug-in's input signal. For now, leave this parameter's default and change it only if VReOrder doesn't respond when you want it to.

7 Start VST from the Left Locator and watch what happens. When the VST song cursor crosses the loop REGION, you'll hear absolutely no-thing. This is because VReOrder first has to sample the audio material. You'll hear its output signal a bar later.

What you have heard up to this point is the original loop, sampled and played back unadulterated, except that of course it is delayed by one bar. Yes, this is not particularly thrilling, but now you can start mangling the signal:

ReOrder ›administers‹ the sampled loop region as sixteen tiny audio snippets. These are represented on the interface via sixteen neighboring columns, each of which you can ma-nipulate individual aspects of.

First set the three SMOOTH parameters at the right to minimum values so the following manipulations are clearly audible. Now try each of these separately:

- LEVEL: Set the second group of columns from the top to a relatively low value. To this end, simply drag the cursor horizontally across the screen. Pull several columns all the way to the top. You can hear that these beats are substantially louder than the others when you play the loop back.

- PANORAMA: In the next lower group of columns, try manipulating the panorama positions in a similar manner.

- REVERSE: In the bottom group of columns you can determine which of the sixteen audio snippets you want the plug to play backwards. In contrast to the previous parameters, which are graduated, these are yes/no or on/off switches.

- POSITION: The top group is the most complicated of the bunch, but also the wackiest. The height of each of the sixteen columns represent their respective sample positions within the loop. This of course means that you can wreak havoc on the sequence in which the sixteen clippings are played back:

1 Start with the defaults.

2 Drag the first column from the left to the fourth box from the bottom—you can always appropriate grandpa's magnifying glass if you have trouble seeing the grid.

3 Then drag the fourth column from the left all the way down.

4 You just swapped the position of the first and fourth audio clipping in the playback sequence. Take a moment to listen to the results. Now imagine how you can use this feature to turn drum loops into completely different grooves!

▶ Note: VReOrder is unable to mix audio snippets internally. It's up to you to make sure that none of the two POSITION columns have identical heights. Otherwise, these are simply played back sequentially rather than simultaneously, which of course has a tendency to confuse the hell out of you when you're playing around with a loop.

If the transition from one snippet to another is too radical for your taste, you can use the SMOOTH parameters mentioned earlier to make the snippets segue more smoothly.

There's one more parameter we haven't discussed, namely FEEDBACK. It lets you variably route the VReOrder output signal back to its input, thus creating a feedback loop. In combination with low DELAY values, you can thus employ VReOrder as you would a ›normal‹ Tempo Delay.

As you can see, VReOrder requires a bit of patience and time, but it's well worth the effort. Keep in mind that there's no law against tinkering with audio material other than drum and percussion loops—this plug is predestined to help you break new sonic ground.

Bo Johansen BJ Flanger

VST Windows	DirectX	—
	VST PC	✓
VST Macintosh		—
Available in VST Racks		Send Effects, Channel Inserts and Master
Standard Routing		Send (Pre-fader) or Insert
World Wide Web		http://www.geocities.com/ SiliconValley/Grid/5051/

BJ Flanger is the latest freeware plug-in by the Danish programer Bo Johansen. To belabor the obvious, it is a chorus/flanger plug-in for VST PC, which can be loaded to any of the VST effects racks and can even be automated.

The first section of the skillfully tailored graphical interface is equipped with faders for the DELAY time and feedback amount. Next comes the LFO modulation section with four selectable waveforms and variable frequency, modulation depth and phase shifting.

Finally, you get a fader each for effects balance and master output level.

The features and user interface of BJ Flanger can give virtually every commercial plug a run for their money, but more importantly, its sound is even better than that of many commercial plugs.

The wide value range of the plug-in's parameters let you coax a great deal more than just conventional chorus and flanger sounds out of it. Fx room simulation, feedback delay, wonky vibrato and even totally bizarro space echoes are possible—and the cool thing is it all sounds pretty wicked.

▶ Here faders are not your only option for manipulating parameters. By clicking on the black center line of a fader, you can change values in smaller increments. But wait, there's more: A click on the numeric value at the bottom end of a fader calls up a utility that looks like a pocket calculator; you can enter numeric values directly to it. This is what I call convenient handling. Bear in mind that this is a freeware plug! Many a professional commercial plug programmer should hang his or her head in shame.

Prosoniq North Pole

VST Windows	DirectX	—
	VST Pc	✓
VST Macintosh		✓
Available in VST Racks		Send Effects, Channel Inserts and Master
Standard Routing		Send (Pre-fader) or Insert
World Wide Web		`http://www.prosoniq.com/`

What do the Prosoniq people, alias Stephan Sprenger and Frederic Schelling, do when they come home in evening, beat from all that commercial plug-in programming? Implausible but apparently true, they program freeware plug-ins.

We'll spare the duo snide comments about the advantages of a social life and the dangers of obsession and put it down to love of craft. The product of this much enthusiasm is called North Pole. This freeware plug-in, now available in a VST Macintosh and VST Pc version (Public Beta), is the virtual replica of an analog synthesizer filter.

▶ On my Macintosh, North Pole had the odd habit of emitting an incredibly annoying whistling noise after if had been running for a good while. It may have been a personal thing, but I would recommend that at least initially you run it at a relatively low volume on your system to keep from shredding its tweeters if your program behaves like mine did.

The left side of the clearly arranged interface grants access to the actual synth filter. MODE lets you select either low- or band-pass characteristics; the standard parameters CUTOFF and RESONANCE are controlled via faders.

I can't remember exactly what (wo)man's basic needs are, but I don't think it was food, shelter and an ENVELOPE FOLLOWER. But who's complaining, it's pretty cool to have anyway. You can fiddle with its ATTACK and RELEASE times as well as modulation intensity (ENV. FOLLOW). Possible sonic trickery includes modulating the cutoff frequency via the input signal level—open sesame, there you have an auto-wah. Just what the doctor ordered to spice up boring drum loops.

Nice and sleazy does it every time, and the North Pole is no exception. Simply tweak the LIST fader to throw a fistful of dirt into the digital gears. If you're still not overwhelmed, how about a complete cross-delay section with faders for the delay effects balance, feedback and delay time? It will deliver up to 1,200 ms, which is sufficient for most timing delays and plenty to impress me.

As you can gather, North Pole is not just your run-of-the-mill filter. With this plug-in, you can make all too clean drum loops sound like anything from slightly greasy to truly scummy. Plus you can make sounds twitch like you zapped them with an unhealthy dose of current or have them waver rhythmically. What's more, all of this stuff sounds stellar. In a nutshell, this is an excellent sonic tool to add ambient waver to your tracks—just the kind of wobble that is up my alley.

North Pole can also be automated—and a good thing this is so. The plug is predestined for remote control mania. Set up dynamic parameter automations for CUTOFF and RESONANCE and be prepared for a wild ride, particularly if you occasionally tweak the delay AM- and FEEDS faders!

Digilogue Blue Line

VST Windows	DirectX	✓
	VST Pc	✓
VST Macintosh	—	
Available in VST Racks	Send Effects, Channel Inserts and Master	
Standard Routing	Send (Pre-fader) or Insert	
World Wide Web	http://members.tripod.de/digilogue/	

BluePhaser

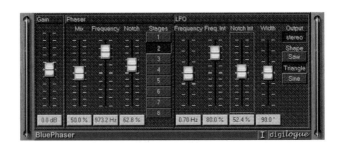

The manuscript for this book was ready for typesetting when I came across the Blue-Line plug-ins by Digilogue, alias Markus Stahlberg. Although my editor may beg to differ, they were definitely worth holding up printing. I'll have to admit when it comes to choosing a plug to highlight, I couldn't decide on which one. To put an end to the vacillation, I settled on briefly introducing you to the entire package. It is available in a VST Pc and DirectX version and comprises the following plugs:

♦ BLUEPHASER: eight-voice phaser with three variable LFO waveforms (sawtooth, triangle, sine)

♦ BLUEFLANGER: flanger with two selectable LFO waveforms and phase shifting

♦ BLUECHORUS: four-voice chorus similar to the flanger, but with less control options

◆ BLUEDELAY: tempo delay, switchable from mono to stereo, with variable high- and low-pass filter. On the second parameter page you can preselect a BPM tempo and use two faders to set the desired note value much like on Dave Brown's Tempo Delay.

◆ BLUEMULTITAP: similar to BlueDelay, but even more complex and convenient. Here you can define up to eight separate delays. After entering a global BPM tempo and a raster value (e.g. $^1/_{16}$) you can move individual taps in a graphic via the mouse and thus influence their levels and delay times.

BlueMultiTap

◆ BLUEPARAMEQ: parametric 4-band EQ with two semiparametric frequency bands without Q and two fully parametric with Q controls. On the second parameter page, frequency response is depicted as a curve. You can edit it directly via mouse like in Waves Q10.

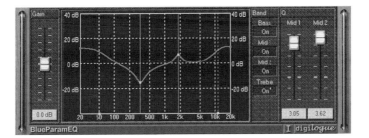

BlueParamEQ

◆ BLUEFILTER: synthesizer filter with different characteristics, slopes and band widths. With the LFO and amplitude follower, you can modulate the frequency or Q-factor of the filter separately. Here too, you'll find a second page offering direct mouse control of the frequency response graphic.

◆ BLUECOMPRESSOR: compressor with all essential parameters, including a graphical representation of the dynamics characteristic curve that can be edited via mouse.

◆ BLUEREVERB: room simulation with six different fundamental characteristics, which can be influenced via four parameters each.

◆ BLUESTEREO: pseudo stereo with separate stereo width and phase manipulation options. Very nice: a variable high-pass filter lets you exclude frequency ranges from manipulations.

◆ BLUEGATE: more than a simple noise gate. Here you can not only control the open and close thresholds separately, but also set up a four-stage amplitude envelope.

All Blue-Line plug-ins make a great initial impression with their graphical interfaces—high marks all around for the groovy look and feel. In some cases, the effects quality is not nearly as impressive. The reverb sounds like its virtual rooms had sheet metal walls—very metallic. The compressor also tends to produce undesirable side effects. The good news is that the delays, filters and modulation effects, i.e. some 80 % of the included plugs, sound great. Their quality is miles ahead of the usual standard for free- or shareware plug-ins!

▶ The Blue-Line plug-ins are shareware. If you like 'em and use 'em regularly—which I'm willing to wager you will—their maker expects that you fork over the shareware fee. Please read the instructions on the CD-ROM for this program. Support your local free- and shareware plug-in makers.

Appendix

CD-ROM Table of Contents

Demo Plug-ins

You can install these demo plug-ins to your VST app to see for yourself what they can do. Follow the manufacturers' installation instructions and you should be good to go.

In contrast to the fully functional versions, the functionality of the demo plug-ins was deliberately curbed to some extent. How the different makers implemented these imaginative little obstructions designed to motivate you into buying the no-holds-barred version differs. Here are a few examples:

Contents for Mac Os

- ◆ Not all of the components are included, as for example with the Hyper Prism demo.

- ◆ A plug squeaks, squawks or makes some annoying noise that reminds you to pay up and run a licensed version.

- ◆ You can't save processing operations, which of course means you can't use the plug for track bouncing.

- ◆ Only a few seconds of a file are processed.

- ◆ The plug has to be started anew every couple of minutes.

- ◆ The plug-in is timed by some type of ›countdown.‹ Either you can only activate it a couple of times or it expires in a few weeks time.

If you give a demo plug-in a trial run and it behaves strangely, this doesn't mean that the fully functional version acts up as well. Be sure to check out the manufacturers' instructions. You'll always find comments on the restrictions of the demo plug-ins.

Contents for Windows

To avoid confusion when you're dealing with the Windows partition of the CD-ROM, the DirectX plug-ins and VST PC plug-ins are distinguished by the labels DX and VST respectively.

Freeware Plug-ins

Here you'll find plug-ins that you can install and use without any restrictions. Nevertheless, these plug-ins are of course the intellectual property of their respective authors. This means that you can't modify them, copy them for commercial purposes or mess with them any other way you can think of without the express written consent of the respective author.

You may have noticed that some of the authors of freeware plug-ins also offer commercial plug-ins. Be sure to check out the Web sites of these freeware authors on the Internet every now and then.

This way you'll see if there's new stuff available and you'll also be helping the authors out—the better frequented a Web site, the more advertising revenue an author can reap.

Helpers

In this folder, you'll find helpful utilities. Next to the Netscape browser, it features software for unpacking files and reading PDF files, and the PC partition is home to several DirectX versions.

Tutorials

This folder holds some multimedia presentations of select plug-ins that demonstrate their features, sounds and user interfaces.

If you own a relatively fast computer and CD-ROM drive, you can start the tutorial applications directly from CD-ROM via a double-click. If your hardware won't cut the mustard, you have no choice but to copy the folder to your hard disk.

WIZOO

Here you'll find the Internet links discussed in this book in HTML format so that you can load these to an Internet browser and then simply click on them. Plus you get the universally coveted current Wizoo catalog in Html format, including excerpts from the other incredibly informative Wizoo Guides.

Vst Plug-ins on the Internet

Here I've compiled a bunch of links to Web sites for you. These will help you get in touch with plug-in makers or provide useful information regarding Cubase Vst. Most links come with a few comments on what they're all about.

The fastest way to go to these sites is to simply open the file vstlinks.htm in the Wizoo folder via your browser and click directly on the links listed there.

The hard-working folks at Wizoo constantly update the Vst links on the Book Support Page at the Wizoo Web site. You'll also find the link to this site on the Cd-Rom in vstlinks.htm.

General Vst Info

Info, help, contacts to other users—here you'll find everything of interest regarding Cubase Vst.

Wizoo

http://www.wizoo.com/

Home of the update pages for this and other Wizoo books. Includes a newbie section with invaluable bilingual (English spoken here) guidance for digital audio and synth novices, a heavily frequented German-language Vst user mailing list and loads more.

Steinberg-Deutschland

http://www.steinberg.de/

German Web site of the Hamburg-based software maker featuring news and information on as well as support and service for Cubase. The company maintains its own Ftp site for fast downloading. First place to go to for users in Germany.

Steinberg Distributors:
http://service.steinberg.de/distributor.nsf
Not all that unexpectedly, a list of all Steinberg distributors.

Steinberg Knowledge Base:
http://service.steinberg.de/sc/knowledge.nsf
Steinberg's own informative and indispensable pages featuring FAQs, particularly on Cubase VST as well as a regularly updated list of all plug-ins that are compatible with Steinberg products.

Cubase Clubs
http://service.steinberg.de/webdoc.nsf/show/club_cubase_d
List of all local Cubase user clubs. I'll bet you thought as much.

Club Cubase Magazine
http://www.steinberg.net/clubcubase/
Online version of the Canadian Cubase Club. Will the alliteration ever cease?

Club Cubase UK
http://www.cix.co.uk/~gal/ccd/
Same, only for current rather than former subjects of the Queen.

Club Cubase LA
http://www.us.steinberg.net/clubcubase.html
More of the same, but since it's in LA and all, maybe you can actually be in the same club as someone who knows someone famous.

Steinberg Training Centre
http://apollo.qcm.gu.edu.au/stc/index.htm
Steinberg site at the Queensland Conservatory of Music: links, plugs, infos.

Cubase for Windows Users

`http://www.studio201.com/cwu/`

Tricks and tips on how to configure Cubase and Vst under Windows, everything about plug-ins, Cubase clubs—coveted mixer maps are also available here.

Cubase Mailing Lists

`http://www.steinberg.de/service/mailinglists.html`

Here you can subscribe to the two extremely popular Vst users mailing lists and talk to like-minded folks every day for the rest of your natural-born life. In addition to the German-language Wizoo Vst list, you'll also find the English-language Cubase List.

Padworld:

`http://www.padworld.demon.co.uk/vst.html`

Info and statistics having to do with configuring Vst Windows.

Cubase Webring—Site List

`http://www.webring.org/cgi-bin/webring?ring=cubase;list`

Association of non-commercial Cubase plug-in makers and Internet sites

Cubase Webring—Registration

`http://www.dbrown.force9.co.uk/webring.html`

Here you can add your site to the Cubase Webring.

Cubase Vst Pc Homepage

`http://www.geocities.com/SiliconValley/Hills/5841`

Bilingual German site (English spoken here) with info, tips, links to freeware plug-ins; in short, the skinny on Vst Windows

Vsт Plug-in Manufacturers

At manufacturer Web sites, you'll not only find current info, but you can also download plug-in updates or the newest demo versions. In many cases, you can buy plug-ins online. Some manufacturers offer a service where when you pay online via credit card, you'll immediately get a number that enables the demo version that you have already installed—in just a matter of seconds, you end up with the fully functional version on your computer.

Aldo Trianti:
http://members.xoom.com/atrianti/start.htm
   Freeware

Antares
http://www.antares-systems.com/
   Auto Tune Vsт

Apogee
http://www.apogee.com/
   Apogee homepage; MasterTools info at Steinberg.

Arboretum
http://www.arboretum.com/
   Hyper Prism Vsт/Dx

Bo Johansen
http://www.geocities.com/SiliconValley/Grid/5051/
   Freeware

Dave Brown
http://www.dbrown.force9.co.uk/
   Tempo Delay, Sweep Delay, Tremolo, Compressor, ProDelay, ProComp

Digilogue
http://members.tripod.de/digilogue
   Freeware

Digital Elements
http://www.digitalelements.be/download.htm
Freeware

Div/Zero
http://www.divzero.com/
Freeware

Duy
http://www.duy.es/
Duy Shape, Max Duy, Duy Wide, DaD Valve

Event/Dsp Fx
http://www.event1.com/
Dsp Fx Virtual Pack

Fraser Stuart
http://www2.one.net.au/~4viewst/vst
Freeware

J. Schmitt
http://www.multimania.com/jeje1999/plug.htm
Freeware (French-language homepage)

Living Memory
http://www.steinberg.de/products/plugins.html
Freeware for Vst Macintosh

Maxim
http://www.abel.net.uk/~maxim/
RingMod, SimpleLi, SoftOver, TestTone

NeuroSonic
http://www.neurosonic-systems.de/
Groove Delay

Object Productions
http://www.vintagefx.com/
Vintage Power Pack Vol. 1

Opcode
http://www.opcode.com/
fusion:Vocode, fusion:Vinyl, fusion:Filter, fusion:Vsт Fx Bundle

Prosoniq
http://www.prosoniq.com/
Voxciter, Roomulator, Ambisone, Dynasone; Freeware North Pole

Q-Sound
http://www.qsound.ca/
Q-Tools

R.S. Plieger
http://www2.hastec.nl/~vstplugins/
Compressor

Sipab
http://www.plugware.com/
Quickverb, Multiverb, Lawn Mover

Sonic Foundry
http://www.sonicfoundry.com/
Noise Reduction, Acoustics Modeler, Xғx 1, Plug-in Pack, Xғx 2, Plug-in-Pack

Spectral-Design
http://www.spectral-design.com/
DeClicker, DeNoiser, Loudness Maximizer, Magneto, Tun-A, Spectralizer, Free-D, Free Filter, Q-Metric, Sᴘʟ De-Esser

Sᴘʟ
http://www.spl-electronics.com/
Sᴘʟ homepage; De-Esser plug-in info at Spectral-Design

Steinberg

http://www.steinberg.net/products/plugins.html

Info and downloads in the Plug-in Zone, not only for Steinberg's own plugs, but also for many VST-compatible plugs by third-party vendors.

Synchromesh

http://www.synchromesh.net/

Freeware

Tc Works

http://www.tcworks.de/

Native Reverb, Native EQ, Native DeX, Native Pack, Native Essentials

Thomas Rehaag

http://www.netcologne.de/~nc-rehaagth/tr.htm

AUM, Spice, PSI—Phase Shift Iterator

Timeworks

http://www.sonictimeworks.com/index.htm

Reverb 4080L, Delay 6022, Phazer Model 88, Mastering EQ

Vellocet

http://vellocet.ii.net/

VPingPong, VFlanger, VNoPhones, VReOrder, VNoiseGate

Vincent Burel

http://webperso.alma-net.net/burel/

QuickVerb, MultiVerb, LawnMover, Stereoizer, D Limiter, Karakao

Waldorf

http://www.waldorf-gmbh.de/

Waldorf homepage; D-Pole plug-in info at Steinberg.

Waves:

http://www.waves.com/

Easy Waves, NPP, L1, Q10, S1, C1, TrueVerb, Maxx Bass, DeEsser, PAZ, Renaissance Compressor, Renaissance EQ

Glossary

This glossary deals primarily with terms, abbreviations and acronyms mentioned in passing in the book, but due to space constraints, weren't explained in detail. There are also a number of terms that you will come across when you are configuring and working with VST. If you can't find a term you're looking for here, check the index.

ADA Convertor—a device that converts an analog signal to a digital signal that represents equivalent information via sampling and vice versa (⇨DA convertors).

   ADAT—digital 8-track audio recorder based on video tape by Alesis; the standard device in its class; diverse generations and models are available.

   ADAT Optical—optical interface for parallel transmission of eight audio channels via fiber-optic cable. Now the established standard for digital multi-channel interfaces.

   AES/EBU—short for ›Audio Engineering Society/European Broadcast Union;‹ this is the association's standard transmission format for professional stereo digital audio signals The format is similar to ⇨S/P-DIF, but uses balanced circuits and higher voltages. Depending on the type of devices involved, AES/EBU and S/P-DIF coax interfaces can in some cases communicate directly.

   Amplitude—term used to describe the amount of a signal. It can relate to volume in an audio signal or the amount of voltage in an electrical signal. In the audio sector, the term is often equated with ›level‹ and ›volume.‹

   ASIO—short for ›Audio Stream Input Output,‹ VST's own software interface to a variety of audio cards.

   Audio File—a file that actually contains digital audio data, as opposed to ⇨audio regions and ⇨audio segments.

   Audio Region—this simulated audio file holds the place for an actual ⇨audio file or portions thereof; it doesn't contain audio data, only peripheral information such as the start and end point.

Aux—short for auxiliary; in mixers, these circuits are usually identical to effects sends.

Bandwidth—general term for the transmission frequency range and thus indicative of audio quality; in conjunction with filters: ⇨Q-factor.

Bus—in computer jargon, this general term refers to data, address and control circuits. The term describes the circuits via which the ⇨Cpu communicates with peripheral devices and expansion cards (⇨Pci, ⇨Nubus).

Bus Width—refers to the maximum number of bits that can be transported via the bus simultaneously, i.e. the de facto number of parallel circuits.

Cd Audio—short for ›Compact Disc—Audio;‹ current standard for stereo music Cds: 44.1 kHz ⇨sampling rate and 16-bit word width

Cd-R—short for ›Cd-Recordable;‹ the term is used for a blank Cd. It is placed in a ⇨Cd-R recorder to burn digital data onto the Cd (cannot be deleted/overwritten).

Cd-R Recorder—also called ›Cd burner‹ or ›toaster;‹ device used to burn data onto ⇨Cd-Rs, can also usually be used as a Cd-Rom drive.

Cd-Rw—short for ›Cd-ReWritable;‹ Similar to ⇨Cd-R, although here data can be deleted and overwritten. Cd-Rw recorders and discs are still relatively expensive.

Clock—frequency specification (usually in MHz) that describes how fast the computer can execute certain operations. The specification for processors is the most widely-known clock type; it pertains to the computing cycle of the ⇨Cpu. Bus clock is also crucial to ⇨performance; it describes at which rate the Cpu can communicate with other computer components via the ⇨busses (›system bus clock‹).

Color Depth—determines how many different colors a computer's graphical system can (and should) display simultaneously. Standard values are 8 bits (256 colors/Low Color), 16 bits (one thousand colors/High Color) and 32 bits (one million colors/True Color). High values give good visuals, but require a great deal of computing performance.

Comb Filter—filter curve with steep notches, which in a graphical representation, resemble the teeth of a comb. Changes the timbre of a sound drastically and is usually considered an undesirable side effect caused by ⇨phase shifting, among others

Cpu—short for ›Central Processing Unit;‹ the main processor that is primarily responsible for the overall performance of the computer.

Cutoff—the frequency at which a filter will start attenuating signals.

Da Conversion—short for ›digital/analog converter;‹ the process that changes an analog signal into a digital signal that represents equivalent information via sampling.

dB—short for ›decibel;‹ a numerical expression for the relative (a logarithmic value) loudness of a sound. Different measures of dB such as dB u or dB V are used depending on the application and nominal value.

Delay—a variable parameter giving the ability to start an event only after a predetermined amount of time. The devices that are used to generate delay signals are also called delays. Can also refer to ⇨runtime discrepancy.

Destructive—›destructive audio processing‹ means that the actual audio data in an ⇨audio file are changed as opposed to just editing peripheral or playback parameters.

Dimm—short for ›Dual In-line Memory Module;‹ board equipped with ⇨Ram memory components; it is plugged into appropriate ⇨slots on the mainboard.

Disk At Once—⇨Cd-R recorder mode: All tracks are written to the ⇨Cd-R without interruption. This mode is generally required to write on Cds in ⇨Cd audio format. Not all ⇨Cd-R recorders can operate in this mode (⇨Track At Once)

Dma—short for ›Direct Memory Access‹—here data transport operations between system components are executed without the help of the Cpu.

Dropout—glitch in an audio signal caused by a brief interruption of the data stream (e.g. faulty DAT tape).

DSP—short for ›Digital Signal Processor,‹ a computer chip designed specifically for computing audio data. This type of chip is installed in some audio cards for computing effects and related data without the help of the CPU.

Duplex—this term goes way back to the days of the telegraph. Today in the context of audio cards, duplex mode refers to parallel operation of audio inputs and outputs. Half-duplex means that an audio card does not support simultaneous recording and playback operation. Full-duplex means that you can use inputs and outputs simultaneously.

DVD—short for ›Digital Versatile Disk,‹ a format that is the designated successor to the contemporary CD (⇨CD audio). These disks store video and audio data. With massive storage capacity of seventeen gigabytes (equivalent to 25 conventional CDs); the format for audio DVD is 24 bits/96 kHz

Early Reflections—term for the initial segment of a reverb or room simulation effects signal, in which individually, audibly separate ›echoes‹ dominate (essential for creating an impression of the size of the simulated room); ⇨reverb tail.

E-IDE—short for ›Enhanced IDE;‹ which is exactly what it actually is, the successor to the ⇨IDE standard.

Enhancer—any device or algorithm that generates additional frequencies that were not originally part of a signal (also called an ⇨exciter).

Envelope—an envelope is a control voltage used to modulate a sound-shaping component within a given time frame so that the sound is changed in some manner. In contrast to an ⇨LFO, this curve is not cyclic, it is unfolds once only. A standard envelope consist of the phases Attack, Decay, Sustain and Release (ADSR).

Envelope Follower—a circuit that follows the level of a signal and converts it into a control voltage, for example to control the ⇨cutoff frequency of a filter (auto-wah).

Exciter—a device—the classic example being the Aphex Exciter—or algorithm that generates additional overtones, allowing lackluster signals to be ›refreshed.‹

FPU—short for ›Floating Point Unit‹—a computer component, subroutine or algorithm that executes floating point calculations. These operations are crucial in real-time audio computing.

Full-duplex—⇨Duplex

Gain—in audio jargon, this term is equivalent to level. For filters, it describes the degree of boost/cut in ⇨dB.

Half-duplex—⇨Duplex

Harmonics—timbre shaping overtones of upper partials that have a specific frequency relationship to the fundamental; the 2nd harmonic is for example dominant in tube distortion, whereas the 3rd harmonic is the prevailing overtone in analog tape saturation.

HFS—›Hierarchical File System,‹ the standard file system of Mac Os.

HFS+—upgrade of HFS introduced with Mac Os 8.1. Most important improvement: HFS+ ensures that small files take up less space on a storage medium. HFS+ is not recommended for audio hard disk. Rather than bringing benefits, it usually causes problems. Current Mac Os versions support HFS and HFS+ formatted media; you can even administer them on the same system if need be.

IDE—short for ›Integrated Device Electronics,‹ a ⇨bus used to connect IDE-compatible devices such as hard disks or CD-ROM drives. The newer standards are Fast ATA 2, ATAPI and ⇨E-IDE.

Insert—a circuit for patching signal processor into the signal path; in contrast to a ⇨send circuit, where the signal is tapped, leaving the original intact and generating a duplicate but processed signal, in an insert, the entire signal is processed. In a VST stereo channel, only a plug-in with stereo-in- and outputs can be used as an insert effect, otherwise only the left channel is processed.

I/O—short for ›Input/Output.‹

Latency—in general, the delay between audio in- and output caused by the time it takes for the system to process these data. In particular, delay between audio and Midi in the Vst audio system.

LFO—short for ›Low Frequency Oscillator;‹ hardware component or algorithm that produces extremely slow oscillations that are used as a ⇨modulation source.

Lo-fi—short for ›low fidelity‹ which means ›poor sound quality;‹ in the world of digital audio this is paradoxically a desirable feature in ⇨vintage or ⇨retro-effects.

LTC—short for ›Longitudinal Time Code‹—synchronization signal for video links that is recorded to a video tape along with images.

Mac Os—short for ›Macintosh Operating System.‹

Mastering—final processing of a completed stereo mixdown to maximize the audio material, for example prior to burning it on CD (which is actually ›pre-mastering,‹ if you wanted to be pedantic about it).

Modulation—in acoustics, a variation in the amplitude, frequency, or phase of a wave in accordance with some signal. A signal or parameter, the ›modulation source,‹ influences another signal or another parameter, the ›modulation destination‹). Modulations animate effects or to some extent shape the modulation destination in the image of the modulation source.

Modulation effects—category of classic effects where a modulation is responsible for generating a given effect. Typical modulation effects include chorus, flanger, phaser, autopan, tremolo.

Non-destructive—›non-destructive audio processing‹ means that the actual audio data in an ⇨audio file are not edited, only peripheral or playback parameters such as ⇨regions and segments.

Nubus—outdated bus format for expansion slots in Macintosh computers. Older models have up to six Nubus slots. The current standard bus format is ⇨Pci.

Pci—short for ›Peripheral Component Interface;‹ Intel ⇨bus standard. Currently the best standard for expansion cards.

Pci Bridge—controller chip via which the Pci bus communicates with the Cpu. In Macintosh-compatible computers with more than three slots, used as a link to the diverse Pci trios.

Pds—short for ›Processor Direct Slot,‹ a slot in many older Macintosh models that is connected directly to the Cpu. It can often be used for a processor upgrade in these models.

Performance—overall computing power determined by the ⇨Cpu, ⇨clock, ⇨Ram and ⇨bus, among other factors.

Phase—also called ›phase position‹ or ›phase angle;‹ specified in values of 0 to 360. It describes an attribute of an oscillation that is especially significant when signals overlap.

Pitch—the element of a tone or sound determined by the frequency of vibration.

Pitch Shifter—normally when audio is played back, tempo and pitch are two sides of the same coin (faster ⇔ higher, slower ⇔ lower). A pitch shifter can defy this natural law and change the pitch of a signal without influencing the tempo (also ⇨time compression/expansion).

Plug-in—modular expansion software that enhance the capabilities of another program. The internal effects in Vst can be upgraded with plug-ins in the requisite format.

Post-fader—here the signal is routed out after the channel volume fader; the send effects signal is influenced by the channel fader.

Power Macintosh—general term for Apple Macintosh computers equipped with a Ppc processor.

Ppq—short for ›Pulses Per Quarter‹—determines how many increments a quarter note is divided into; essential for sequencer timing, among others.

Pre-delay—in a room simulation, the interval before the first ⇨early reflections become audible (essential for creating an impression of the size of the simulated room).

Pre-fader—here the signal is routed out before the channel volume fader; the send effects signal is not influenced by the channel fader. Normally the fader is pulled all the way down to mute the dry signal completely.

Q-factor—(Q=quality) determines the width of the affected frequency range. A high Q-factor defines a narrow band and a low Q-factor a wide band. Related terms are ›bandwidth‹ and ›slope.‹

RAM—short for ›Random Access Memory.‹ This is the memory that handles your working data; its capacity is expressed in MB (megabytes). Normally this memory is ›volatile,‹ which means that the contents are only saved for as long as the device is powered up.

Resonance—self-oscillation; a ›resonance-capable‹ filter can significantly color a timbre (make it sound hollow, chirp, squeak, whistle), much more than a filter without resonance. For synthesizers and sound design this type of filter is considered the standard.

Resources—term for the global performance capability of a computer; depends on a number of factors, ⇨CPU and ⇨RAM among others.

Retro—in the context of effects, this term refers to emulations of ›vintage‹ sounds or devices which are now back in vogue. Desirable attributes include tube tone, lo-fi, crackling, hiss and so forth. Retro sounds are prevalent in trip hop and ambient styles.

Reverb Tail—term for the final stage of a reverb or room simulation effects signal in which the individual ›echoes‹ merge into a diffuse whole; ⇨early reflections.

Ring modulation—mathematically, multiplication of two signals; produces distorted to metallic sounds.

Routing—generally sending signals from point to another, assigning in- and outputs and so forth.

Run-time discrepancy—minimal delay of audio signals, usually in the millisecond range. Generally not a huge problem expect for with signals that are linked directly (e.g. the two channels in a stereo recording. In this case, these differences generate phase shifting and ⇨comb filter effects.

Sample Rate—also called ⇨sampling frequency. The term describes the frequency at which analog audio material is sampled.

Sample Rate Converter—device or algorithm that translates one ⇨sample rate into another; this conversion always leads to some type timing problem—the quantizing goes out of whack, which degrades the audio quality.

SDRAM—›Synchronous Dynamic Random Access Memory;‹ a special type of D⇨RAM. In addition to conventional control signals, it works with a clock signal for faster access. SDRAM is used in Apple's current G3 computers D⇨RAM.

Send—in contrast to an ⇨insert, here only part of a signal is tapped and routed to an effect. The VST Send Effects rack works with a mono input and stereo output. (also ⇨Pre-fader and ⇨Post-fader).

Sidechain—separate independent signal circuit for controlling an effect (e.g. for a de-esser).

SIMM—short for ›Single In-line Memory Module;‹ board with ⇨RAM modules that is plugged into the corresponding ⇨slots on the computer's mainboard.

Slot—general term for the expansion ports on the computer's mainboard.

S/P-DIF—short for ›Sony/Philips Digital InterFace;‹ standard format for transporting digital audio data. Either an optical or a coaxial interface, depending on the type of device. The format is similar to AES/EBU, although it features unbalanced circuits and lower voltages. Nevertheless, AES/EBU and S/P-DIF coax interface can often communicate directly (depending on the type of devices involved).

Tap—term for a single echo or reflection; in the specifications for a delay, it describes the number of echoes it can generate simultaneously (›multi-tap‹).

TDIF—short for ›Tascam Digital Interface Format;‹ a digital 8-channel interface that is primarily used for connecting digital multi-track recorders (DTR) by Tascam.

Terminator—in a ⇨Scsi system, the first and last device in the chain have to be equipped with an activated terminating resistor; available as a switchable internal component or an external connector designed to fit the Scsi port.

Time Compression—feature that enables faster audio playback speeds without influencing pitch (also ⇨time compression/expansion).

Time Expansion—feature that enables slower audio playback speeds without influencing pitch (also ⇨time compression/expansion).

Track At Once—⇨Cd-R recorder mode: Each track is written individually to the ⇨Cd. The laser that is doing the writing is switched off at the end of a track and switched on again at the start of the next track (⇨Disk At Once).

Track Bouncing—general term describing the process by which a track is recorded from the audio output to the audio input of the same device or program to condense tracks or compute effects into tracks. In VST, this function is accessible via the CREATE FILE button in the Master section.

Transients—extremely brief signal peaks, for instance a kick drum impulse with a great deal of ›snap.‹

USB—›Universal Serial Bus;‹ Intel-sponsored standard for communication between computers and peripherals. The serial circuit between devices via a single, low-cost cable slows data transport down, so it is unsuitable for audio hard disks. First integrated in an Apple computer with the release of iMac.

Vintage—general term for older, usually valuable musical instruments and studio devices, or classic sounds (⇨retro).

VRAM—short for ›Video Random Access Memory;‹ fast memory on graphics cards for buffering screen contents.

Wordclock—clock signal required by digital audio interfaces to ensure the sampling rates of the connected devices run in absolute sync.

And this Year's Wizoos Winners Are ...

...Tom Wendt, Manfred Rürup, Charlie Steinberg, Stefan Scheffler, Mert Ergün and Dave Nicholson of Steinberg for innovation, gracious support and allowing me to gaze into the Steinberg crystal ball,

all plug-in manufacturers mentioned herein for their friendly support,

Gisela Derichs for untiring assistance,

Uwe Senkler for text mastering above and beyond the call of duty,

Peter Gorges as ›The Big Wizoo‹ for vodka-no-lemon cocktails, conscientious pool maintenance and innovative hair design.

Index